CASE STUDIES IN
CULTURAL ANTHROPOLOGY

GENERAL EDITORS
George and Louise Spindler
STANFORD UNIVERSITY

PADJU EPAT
The Ma'anyan of Indonesian Borneo

D1501400

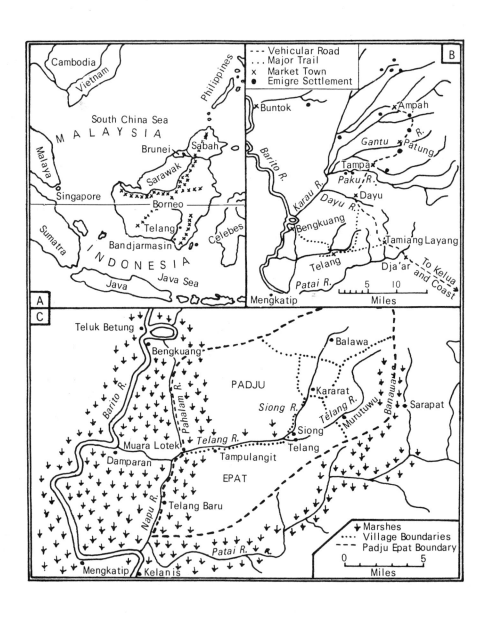

PADJU EPAT
The Ma'anyan of Indonesian Borneo

By
A. B. HUDSON
Michigan State University

HOLT, RINEHART AND WINSTON, INC.
NEW YORK   CHICAGO   SAN FRANCISCO   ATLANTA
DALLAS   MONTREAL   TORONTO   LONDON   SYDNEY

This book is dedicated to the memory of
Claire Holt

Cover: Harvesting rice

Foreword

About the Series

These case studies in cultural anthropology are designed to bring to students, in beginning and intermediate courses in the social sciences, insights into the richness and complexity of human life as it is lived in different ways and in different places. They are written by men and women who have lived in the societies they write about and who are professionally trained as observers and interpreters of human behavior. The authors are also teachers, and in writing their books they have kept the students who will read them foremost in their minds. It is our belief that when an understanding of ways of life very different from one's own is gained, abstractions and generalizations about social structure, cultural values, subsistence techniques, and the other universal categories of human social behavior become meaningful.

About the Author

A. B. Hudson is an Associate Professor of Anthropology at Michigan State University. He received his undergraduate education at Harvard and Berkeley, and his Ph.D. from Cornell (1967), where he minored in linguistics and Southeast Asian Studies. He carried out anthropological field research in Indonesian Borneo from January 1963 to June 1964, under a grant from the Ford Foundation Foreign Area Training Program. More recently, between July 1969 and June 1970, he conducted a survey of indigenous languages in Indonesian and Malaysian Borneo and in Brunei, with the assistance of a grant from the American Council of Learned Societies.

About the Book

This brief case study provides a tight and comprehensive description of the way of life of the Padju Epat Ma'anyan, an important people of Indonesian Borneo, an area underrepresented in the more available anthropological sources. The author most notably accomplishes several purposes.

He presents one of the most complete descriptions of swidden technology and its wider social, economic, and ecological dimensions. These inter-relationships are complex, but the author has pursued them with great clarity. The documentation and illustration provided by the Padju Epat case make it possible for the student to understand this most important form of adaptation.

v

The case study also gives us a dynamic treatment of the relationships between the *adat* legal system, religious beliefs, and religious groupings. The description of the adjudication process shows us how the legal system operates as a mechanism of social control and shows how it has the potential for adapting to changing conditions.

Dr. Hudson's discussion of the kin-group system in Padju Epat is also of particular significance. His treatment is, again, dynamic in that he shows the determinants of structural variability in kin-group types and describes changes, both cyclical and linear, over time. The author's discussion of kindred ties and kindred activities and the relationship between the *bumuh* descent group and kindred is a model of clarity. Beginning students will find this section challenging, but it is laid out so clearly that by careful study its functions and structural interrelationships will become understandable.

It is also helpful to have emphasized in this book that the people of Padju Epat live in the twentieth century, and although somewhat isolated spatially, they are tied socially, economically, and politically to the outside world.

The case study represents cultural anthropology well as a discipline. It provides the student with a solid illustration of the way in which basic analytic principles can be applied to a body of data. The case study has very little redundancy in it and deserves a careful reading.

GEORGE AND LOUISE SPINDLER
General Editors

Stanford in Germany
March 1971

Contents

Introduction

PADJU EPAT IS A SMALL SUBDISTRICT located in the interior of the southern part of Borneo, in Indonesia's province of Central Kalimantan. It is situated, as the crow flies, about one hundred miles north of the populous coastal city of Bandjarmasin. A few miles west lies the great southward flowing Barito River. Although the region's traditional name, Padju Epat, literally means "four villages," there are at present six villages in the subdistrict: Telang, Siong, Murutuwu, Kararat, Balawa, and Tampulangit. In 1964, Padju Epat's entire population was about 1,100.

With the exception of the villagers of Tampulangit, the people of Padju Epat belong to the Ma'anyan Dayak tribe, a group numbering between thirty and thirty-five thousand who are spread through much of the southeastern watershed of the Barito River. The Ma'anyan have a distinctive Dayak language, a common set of traditions, and are primarily animist or Christian in religion. By contrast, the 240 residents of Tampulangit are Bandjar Malays, an ethnic group of over a million whose distribution is concentrated in the coastal regions of southern Borneo. The Bandjars speak a Malay language and are strong adherents of the Moslem religion.

Life in Padju Epat is quiet. It is an isolated region, separated from the outside world by marshes to the east, south, and west. No vehicular roads lead to Padju Epat's villages, and boat travel is practical only during the rainy months each year. With the exception of market day, held once a week in Telang, visitors to Padju Epat are infrequent, and no outsiders choose to settle there. Nearly all of Padju Epat's population was born in one or another of its villages, while many of its families have left the subdistrict, for the soil is poor and its moribund seclusion has proven dispiriting. Each year a few more people join the long list of emigres who have left the area in recent decades to seek better farming land in the north.

The villages themselves are small, with populations ranging between 120 and 250 inhabitants, except for the tiny hamlet of Kararat, where 35 people live in only two houses. Thus in Padju Epat the villager never experiences the teeming crowds associated with Asian city life, but spends his days in the quiet company of his family, relatives and friends. Yet he is gregarious by nature and delights in social events that attract throngs of people. Despite the isolated circumstances in Padju Epat, most villagers are not ignorant of the modern world. Most men, and many women, have traveled extensively through-

1

out southern Borneo, some to continue their education, some to seek their fortunes, and others to visit relatives in distant communities. Many speak several languages in addition to their native Ma'anyan, and nearly everyone knows some Indonesian, the official national language.

For his subsistence, the Padju Epat villager follows a traditional way of life, cultivating dry rice in swidden plots. Using a slash and burn technique, the cultivator first fells trees in the forest, then burns his clearing before planting his rice. Drenching rains quickly remove nutriments from the region's poor soil, forcing the Padju Epater to abandon old swidden fields after a year or two. New fields must be cut with enormous effort, and old ones left for ten to fifteen years until secondary forest cover has regenerated enough to support crops once more. The Padju Epater supplements his subsistence by fishing, hunting and forest gathering; the cultivation of rubber trees provides him supplementary cash income.

Villagers spend much of the year far from the main settlements, tending the fields they have carved from the equatorial forest. Since new fields must be cut at the beginning of each agricultural year, the distribution of swiddens about the village territory changes considerably from year to year. A family may pass one agricultural season in virtual seclusion, far from the village or any other farms. The next year, they may join with several other families to form a small hamlet in which the individual plots and field houses are close together. Such a temporary hamlet provides its resident families with greater scope for cooperation and sociability, yet sometimes the close association breeds conflict as well.

The months of hard work in the swidden are punctuated by periods of festivity. During the agricultural season, cooperative work groups bring conviviality to the arduous labor of clearing, burning, planting, and harvesting the swidden fields. Community fish drives, too, are gay occasions. Ceremonies sponsored by families to commemorate the births, marriages, and deaths of their members are celebrated by public feasting and story telling. Each year after the rice is harvested, the main village settlements come to life as inhabitants return from their distant swiddens. Every household bustles with activity as its members host various thanksgiving and spirit propitiation ceremonies. Every Tuesday, a market is held in Telang. When there is high water during the rainy season, boats come in from the Barito River, and Telang is thronged with people. Occasionally on the eve of market day, an all night dancing and singing session is held. But after the rains end, and the river gets low, market attendance drops, and village life again ebbs as families return to the forest to clear their swidden plots for the new agricultural year.

Although the Padju Epater works hard for his living, his life offers many different activities to the individual, allowing satisfying scope for the indulgence of his whims and proclivities. On any given day a man may choose to hunt, fish, weed his fields, work on a canoe, cut shingles for his roof, tap his rubber trees, or any one of a host of other activities. All must eventually be done, but with few exceptions, the individual has a great deal of immediate choice as to when, where, and how these tasks are to be carried out. With part of each year focused on the main village settlement and part on the swiddens, there is seasonal variety in one's place of residence. Some people spend almost every night in the village, while others are rarely seen there, instead staying in their distant swidden plots throughout the year. Everybody at every season, no matter where he spends the night, frequently walks back and forth between swidden and village. As each family relocates its plots and main field house annually, there is potential variety in swidden neighbors. Among kinsmen, an individual may choose to maintain close relations with some and virtually ignore others. Padju Epaters may even choose to leave the district entirely in the search for better land. In the rhythm of shifting cultivation, there is little difficulty in moving to an entirely new locale at the beginning of a new agricultural year, especially if one already has kinsmen resident there.

Padju Epaters are extremely interested in their own customs and traditions, and spend a fair amount of time studying and discussing them in a rather academic way. They also take a lively interest in other people's ways of doing things. Widely traveled Padju Epaters will sit around of an evening comparing the ways in which different groups organize their lives and handle social problems. Since they themselves take such an interest in human customs, they did not think it unreasonable that an anthropologist and his wife should come half-way around the world to study theirs. They were most cooperative, and even insistent that we get out and see everything for ourselves. No local legal case would begin until we had arrived, and as my notes on legal decisions grew, I found myself cast into the role of an adjudicating elder because of my knowledge of precedents. Most of my questions were answered with alacrity, but in keeping with their own interests, Padju Epaters had questions of their own about American customs. How did we handle problems of fruit stealing, tree burning, inheritance, unwed motherhood, and old age? Sometimes, I had the feeling I was failing in my duties as an informant, for occasionally my answers would be met by a sympathetic grunt, a polite bobbing of the head, or a rather incredulous expression.

During our fourteen months in Padju Epat, we acquired a host of friends and a mountain of data. The material presented in this small work is intended to introduce the reader to the world of the Padju Epat villager, his community, his mode of subsistence, his relations with spirits, kinsmen, and neighbors, and his connections with the outside world.

The Island of Borneo

BORNEO, THE WORLD'S THIRD LARGEST ISLAND, lies in the equatorial seas of insular Southeast Asia. Located southwest of the Philippines, west of Celebes, north of Java, east of Singapore, and southeast of Vietnam, the island spans some 775 miles from north to south (about the distance between San Francisco and Seattle), 725 miles from east to west, and measures about 288,000 square miles in area (greater than the combined areas of California, Oregon, and half of Washington). In 1961 the island had a population of 5.4 million people.

The island's territory is divided among three countries. In the southern three-fifths of the island lie the four Indonesian provinces of East Kalimantan (78,100 sq. mi.; 551,000 population), South Kalimantan (14,530 sq. mi.; 1,473,000 population), Central Kalimantan (58,900 sq. mi.; 497,000 population), and West Kalimantan (56,000 sq. mi.; 1,581,000 population). Along the central northwest coast lies the tiny Sultanate of Brunei (2,226 sq. mi.; 83,877 population), a protectorate state in the Commonwealth of Nations. To the east and west of Brunei respectively, are the Malaysian states of Sabah (29,388 sq. mi.; 454,421 population) and Sarawak (48,250 sq. mi.; 744,529 population).

The island is almost bisected by the equator. The Bornean landscape is dominated by a lush tropical vegetation, most of it in the form of virgin forest, and by a system of innumerable rivers and streams that rise in the mountainous interior regions and debouch into the various seas that surround the island: the Sulu Sea, the Celebes Sea, the Macassar Strait, the Java Sea, and the South China Sea. Both the vegetation and the rivers are sustained by a heavy rainfall that, with regional variations, averages between 80 and 200 inches annually (among United States cities the maximum is 68 inches in Mobile, the minimum 7 inches in Reno; more typical annual averages are 20 inches in San Francisco and 42 inches in Boston). Borneo receives considerable rainfall from towering cumulonimbus cloud formations, often seven or eight miles in depth, generated by the extensive vertical air convection systems common to equatorial regions.

The Monsoon Pattern

Like most of the islands in Southeast Asia, Borneo experiences a double monsoon, a rainfall pattern in which the direction of the prevailing, rain-bearing winds shifts semiannually in response to seasonal changes far away in the interior of mainland Asia. In the spring and summer months of the northern hemisphere, the intense rays of the sun heat the central Asian land, and, by reflection, its overlying air mass. The heated air then rises, creating an extensive low pressure area into which cooler air flows in an anticyclonic pattern. This massive air flow affects Borneo from May to September as a southerly wind, termed the southern monsoon. The southern monsoonal winds approach the island's south coast from the southeast, following the counterclockwise cyclonic pattern of the southern hemisphere winter, and after crossing the equator they are deflected toward the northeast in conformity with the counterclockwise anticyclonic pattern of the northern hemisphere. Consequently this airflow is usually termed the "southeast monsoon" in the southern part of the island, and the "southwest monsoon" in the northern part. As the southern monsoon wind approaches Borneo, it absorbs large quantities of moisture while crossing the eastern extension of the Indian Ocean and the Java Sea. Much of the moisture is then precipitated in the form of drenching rain as the monsoon wind moves across Borneo. In the northern hemisphere's fall and winter months, this giant weather machine reverses itself. The cold central Asian land chills the overlying air, which descends, creating a massive high pressure area and generating air movements southward. The air flow affects Borneo from October to March as northerly winds, and is termed the northern monsoon. Again, the equator deflects the direction of the wind pattern so that it is usually called the "northeast monsoon" in the northern portion of the island, and the "northwest monsoon" in the southern part. As the northern monsoon wind approaches Borneo across the South China Sea, it too absorbs large amounts of moisture which are deposited as rain over the island. In the three or four week period intervening between the two monsoonal phases, Borneo receives a brief respite from recurrent rainfall.

Although the double monsoon pattern is one of the major climatological features of the island as a whole, different regions of Borneo experience variations in the master pattern caused by local geographical conditions. Mountain ranges of differing heights and orientations are the most important geographical feature affecting local variations in the monsoonal pattern.

Most of southern, western, and northwestern Borneo lies below 600 feet in elevation. However, a complex network of interior mountain ranges extends diagonally across the island from the northeast, where the truncated mass of Mt. Kinabalu soars over 13,000 feet into the sky, to the southwest, where Mt. Raya forms a 7,474 foot anchor. From the center of this great diagonal system, the less lofty Klingkang Range, with peaks rising 2,000 to 4,000 feet, runs westward to the island's northwestern cape to form part of the border between Malaysian Sarawak and Indonesian Borneo. In the southeastern part of the island, and relatively detached from the central mountain network, lies the Meratus Range with a north–south axis and peaks of from 3,500 to 6,200 feet in height. This latter range lies some 60 miles to the east of Padju Epat.

In some areas, a mountain range acts as a barrier to the passage of heavy, moisture-laden monsoonal air currents, creating a dry rain shadow to leeward. As the approaching moist air mass is forced upward by the slope of the mountain range, its temperature cools, precipitating most of the moisture as torrential rainfall on the windward side. After crossing the height of land with much of its moisture already lost, the monsoonal air current blows off the mountains as a warm, dry wind, termed a foehn, from which little or no rain falls on the leeward side. Thus, despite the overall rainy character of the island's climate, some regions may experience dry periods ranging up to six months in duration. In Padju Epat there is an extended dry season between June and October when the district is exposed to a foehn blowing off the Meratus Range during the southeast monsoon.

Borneo experiences relatively warm, though not excessively hot weather throughout the year. The average annual temperature is about 80° F. in the coastal areas where permanent weather stations are maintained, and perhaps up to ten to fifteen degrees cooler in the highland regions where weather conditions are not normally recorded. Because of the island's equatorial location, its temperatures do not vary much throughout the year. Generally, the hottest month averages two degrees warmer, and the coldest month two degrees cooler than the annual average for a particular region. There is an average daily temperature range of about twelve to fifteen degrees, fluctuating in the coastal areas from a high of about 90° at midday, to a low in the mid-70's at night. Only rarely does the mercury climb above 95° in any region, and an early morning temperature of 43°, recorded at an altitude of 5,500 feet, is about the lowest figure that has ever been reported.

Soils and the Swidden Cycle

Borneo's luxuriant vegetation belies a rather poor soil base. The central mountain ranges have granitic cores; in the northern and eastern portions of the island there are extensive sandstone and limestone formations in the folds of which some important petroleum fields have been found. With the exception of a few isolated regions in Sabah to the northeast, there are no traces of recent volcanic activity in Borneo. Thus the island lacks this source of potential soil fertility that is so characteristic of the neighboring regions of Sumatra, Java, Bali, Celebes, and the Philippines.

In Borneo's hot, moist equatorial climate, the twin forces of bacterial

A swidden field at planting time.

action and chemical leaching have combined to produce impoverished soils, poor in both organic and inorganic plant nutrients. The warm, humid conditions stimulate intensive bacterial activity that inhibits the formation of more than a very thin humus layer beneath the forests that cover most of the island. Any organic material that accumulates on the forest floor, such as fallen leaves, trees, or animal remains, is rapidly broken down by bacterial action into nutrients that are almost immediately reabsorbed by living plants. As a result, very few organic nutrients are held in the soil as humus, so that this layer is rarely more than a few inches deep. Many nonorganic mineral nutrients necessary for the sustenance of plant life are removed from the upper layers of the soil by a process of chemical leaching. Warm rainwater percolating downward through the soil generates chemical reactions that remove the soluble bases and silicates, leaving behind a relatively infertile mixture of iron oxides and clay, termed laterite. Lateritic soils have a wide distribution in humid tropical and equatorial regions; they take the form of either red or yellow clay, depending on the degree of hydration of the iron oxides present. Thus, the forest soil of Padju Epat consists of an inch or two of humus over a deep lateritic clay base.

Because of the infertility of the lateritic soil base, most forest plants and trees have very shallow but extensive root systems that make possible the rapid reabsorption of accumulated organic nutrients broken down by bacterial action. As a result, most organic nutrients are locked up in living forms rather than in the soil where they would be exposed to loss by chemical leaching. Despite the thin humus and lateritic base, then, the forest can be maintained in a biotic equilibrium established by the rapid recycling of organic nutrients among living forms.

However, the equilibrium is upset when the forest is cleared for swidden plots. When the tree cover is removed, the soil is exposed directly to the hot rays of the equatorial sun and the full, unbroken force of the monsoon rains. Under these conditions, the forces of bacterial action and chemical weathering, already intense, are greatly increased, and the marginal soil rapidly deteriorates in quality. If the clearing has been made on a steep slope, the deleterious effects of erosion are added to the other factors destroying the biotic equilibrium. In addition, with the humus-producing forest cover removed, there is no immediate source for regeneration of soil fertility. Consequently, a forest swidden plot becomes unfit for agricultural use after a year or two and should be abandoned. In hilly areas where the effects of erosion are most strongly felt, plots are usually abandoned after only one year's use. In regions that have a flat or gently rolling topography, such as Padju Epat, swidden plots may be used for two, and sometimes three years, but each successive year of use gives progressively lower agricultural yields. Usually, by the third year, the anticipated harvest from a plot is too small to be worth the expenditure of seed and the effort of planting.

The number of years that must be allowed to pass before an abandoned plot may be reused depends on the amount of time it takes for the regeneration of secondary forest on the site. For the forest, in the form of its humus and ash residue, is the ultimate source of the minimal soil fertility necessary to support swidden agriculture. Only the forest floor is sufficiently protected from the direct forces of heat and rain to allow the accumulation of even a thin layer of humus. Although some humus is destroyed when a newly cleared field is burned over, some remains to provide crop nourishment. However, the greatest source of crop nutriment comes from the ash deposit that remains after the firing of the felled forest. Thus, the speed of forest regeneration dictates the ideal length of time that should pass before an abandoned swidden plot may be reused for farming.

The rate of forest regeneration depends upon the number of successive years a plot has been used before abandonment. In the system of Bornean swidden agriculture, every plot, whether in its first, second, or third year of use, is burned to remove brush, weeds, and other debris. In second and third year plots no humus remains, but the fields gain some fertilization from the ash residue of the annual burning. However, while successive burnings may provide some immediate fertility, they also upset the balance of survival potential between tree and weed species. In a plot cleared from mature forest and used only one year before abandonment, small trees and shrubs begin to spring up within a few months from seedlings and root suckers. Some ferns and grasses also appear, but these soon disappear as spreading tree foliage occludes their sunlight. In fields burned a second year, the fire destroys not only most of the newly emergent tree shoots, but, in the absence of protective humus, the seeds of their species as well. In contrast, vast quantities of feather-light weed seeds and spores, that can drift for miles on the gentlest breezes, settle on the plot; since these are fire resistant, they are not destroyed by the burning. Fewer trees and shrubs survive to inhibit the growth of weeds, and with each successive burn, the weeds take a more commanding position in the field, depriving the tree seedlings of whatever nutrients remain in the soil. The relatively heavy tree seeds will blow only short distances, with the result that once their sucker shoots, seedlings, and seeds have been killed by fire on a given site, these species are not easily reestablished there. Thus, with each successive burning the weeds become more dominant, and the period required for forest regeneration progressively longer.

Allowing for variations in local topographic, rainfall, and soil conditions, the forest on a site that has been farmed for only one, or at most two years, will have regenerated to the point where it can be recleared after some twelve to twenty years. Provided that sufficient periods for forest regeneration are allowed, a second order biotic equilibrium will be established and a given region may support a viable, rotating swidden system in perpetuity. However, if it is the local practice to allow insufficient time before reclearing swidden sites, there will be such progressive soil impoverishment over the years that eventually the forest will not come back and the sites will be unproductive, forcing their abandonment for perhaps generations to come.

Sometimes the balance between weeds and trees is so upset that the forest never comes back. In various parts of Borneo there are vast tracts of savanna covered only by the hardy grasses of genus *Imperata*, which spring from light, wind-blown seeds and can grow in extremely marginal soils. Their exclusive presence in a plot or larger area signals the penultimate stage in soil degeneration. These grasses have no economic value, since they are too coarse to be used for the grazing of animals. A number of areas in Padju Epat support only this kind of growth. If a fire should burn off the *Imperata* grass cover from a tract, the ultimate stage in soil destruction may be reached. Heavy rainfall may so destroy the soil's character as to make it an inviable base for even hardy weeds. The texture of the uppermost layer of laterite is broken down, leaving a surface covering of the purest sand in which nothing will grow. Although it may seem anomalous in an area noted for lush equatorial vegetation, many overswiddened regions in Borneo, including Padju Epat, exhibit stretches of sand of a quality usually associated with the finest bathing beaches.

Although not limited to those areas, savannas are more common in the regions of Borneo that experience an extended dry season during the time that swidden plots are being cleared and burned. In Padju Epat the debris in a field may have been exposed to no rain at all for several months prior to burning. Under such dry conditions, burning is very efficient, a factor that provides a fairly good deposition of fertile ash. However, since fire is the most effective agent upsetting the tree–weed balance, grasses have a better chance to become established under these conditions, so that the short term benefits of efficient burning are potentially offset by long term deleterious effects.

In regions that have a double rainy season, successful burning is a chancy thing usually carried out in the short, relatively dry interval between the southern and northern monsoons. Here, field debris may have only a week or two to dry out before firing, and often an unexpected rainstorm will ruin the chances both for an adequate burn and for the deposition of its fertile ash residue. Each year, people living in such areas are forced to decide whether to burn a fairly dry field early, or to wait longer, hoping for a somewhat drier field but at the risk of an inadequate burn should a sudden rainshower fall. Burning in these areas, however, is not so destructive of soil fertility as it is in Padju Epat.

There are two major factors that may influence people to reclear abandoned swidden sites before adequate forest regeneration has taken place. The first is related to ease of clearing, for it is easier to clear secondary forest trees of seven to ten years' growth, than those twelve to twenty years old. Human nature being what it is, some families in some years will elect to clear plots from secondary forest that has insufficiently regenerated to maintain a perpetual swidden cycle. Secondly, in some areas, population densities may reach such a high level that forests must be cut prior to the achievement of adequate regeneration.

Unfortunately, there is very little information available now concerning the maximum population densities that a swidden system will support without upsetting the equilibrium. Estimates have ranged from 50 to 130 persons per square mile, with a hypothetical density of from 50 to 60 persons per square mile reported in a Sarawak study.

However, the annual agricultural land needs of a Bornean family may vary considerably, even within a single community. The quality of the soil, the topographic profile of the land, the relative importance of hunting and fishing in the local economy, the subsistence and ceremonial requirements for cultigens, are all factors that exhibit considerable variation. In addition, the introduction of rubber cultivation in many areas over the last fifty years has added a new factor, for plots planted in rubber are not usually recleared during the productive life of the trees, which may span thirty, forty, or more years. The rubber trees help to maintain the soil but they take potential agricultural land out of circulation, causing remaining farm sites to be used more intensively. Finally, not all parts of a community's territory may be arable. Marshes unfit for cultivation often form in low-lying areas. In Padju Epat, as well as in many other districts within a hundred miles of the southern or western coasts, the land gradient is so gentle that floodwaters backing up from major rivers often cover considerable areas during the monsoon, rendering them useless for normal agricultural purposes. Once overswiddening has begun to affect a region, the presence of savannas and sandy patches may further diminish the area of cultivable land within the territory of a community. And while a community's gross area may be calculated fairly accurately from a map, the amount of arable land is not so easily determined. In

Padju Epat, for instance, the gross population density is about 10 people per square mile. Yet I have estimated on the basis of my trips through Padju Epat territory that well over 30 percent of the district's 112 square miles is unsuitable for cultivation, so that the effective density per square mile of arable land is about 17 people. Even with this low figure, Padju Epat land has a worn-out appearance, leading one to surmise that its population density may have been much greater in the past before extensive emigration from the district began.

The People

Like Padju Epat, Borneo as a whole is rather sparsely populated. The island's 5.4 million inhabitants are distributed over 288,000 square miles, giving an average population density of about 19 per square mile. Yet, as one might expect, the population is not evenly distributed throughout Borneo. There are concentrations of population in and near the coastal towns that serve as trade and administrative centers. In addition, there are a few regions where geographical conditions permit sedentary flood plain agriculture in rich alluvial soils, supporting population densities above 300 per square mile. In the Central Hulu Sungai regency of South Kalimantan, where the middle reaches of the Negara River are ideal for irrigated agriculture, the population density is about 360 per square mile, a figure that approximates that of New York State. On the other hand, there are regions deep in the island's interior that are practically uninhabited, and where population density runs under 1 per square mile. Great disparities emerge even when comparing entire provinces or states of Borneo. At the low end of the scale, the Indonesian province of East Kalimantan has a population density of only 7 per square mile (about equivalent to that of Idaho), while at the upper end, South Kalimantan has an overall density of 101 per square mile (equal to Florida). However, the latter figure is not representative, for the second and third highest population density figures, for Brunei and West Kalimantan, are only 38 per square mile (equal to Arkansas) and 28 per square mile (equal to Maine) respectively. In general, then, except where special conditions exist, population densities over most of Borneo are low.

Borneo's population, while not as ethnically diverse as that found in the countries of mainland Southeast Asia, is quite heterogeneous. The vast majority of the island's peoples can be assigned to one of three general categories: Chinese, Malay, or Dayak.

About 14 percent of the island's population is of Chinese ancestry. The main concentrations of Chinese are found in the northern and western regions of Borneo, where they constitute more than 20 percent of the populations of Sabah (23%), Brunei (26%), Sarawak (30%) and West Kalimantan (20%). In the remaining Indonesian provinces of Central, South and East Kalimantan, Chinese comprise less than 3 percent of the population. However, this category itself is not homogeneous, for there is considerable linguistic, economic, and cultural variability within the Chinese community, reflecting the considerable diversity in China's Kwangtung and Fukien provinces, whence most Southeast Asian Chinese derive their origins. The people of Padju Epat have little contact with Chinese, since in the southeastern region of the island, the Chinese population is largely restricted to the cities.

The Malay segment constitutes about 41 percent of Borneo's population. The term Malay is used in a general way to cover all Moslems of Indonesian origin, most of whom speak a Malay language. Between the fourteenth and eighteenth centuries, the Malays spread from their homeland in south Sumatra and the Malay Peninsula, to settle along the coasts and larger rivers of Borneo and other Indonesian islands. During their period of expansion, the Malays played an active role, both in the development of the Indies' burgeoning spice trade and in the propagation of Mohammedanism, with the result that Malay became established throughout the archipelago both as a commercial *lingua franca* and as the cultural language of Islam. Where Malay trading communities were established, Malay settlers followed and, adapting themselves to the local conditions, engaged not only in trade but in farming, fishing, and other noncommercial pursuits as well. In the course of time, the different Malay settlements in Borneo absorbed an influx of emigres in varying numbers from the coastal regions of north Java, Macassar, and other areas. Local variants of the basic Malay culture have developed in the different regions of Borneo, and each has come to be distinguished by a particular name and dialect.

To further increase the heterogeneity of the Malay category, over the centuries many of Borneo's indigenous peoples have converted to Islam. Of these autochthonous Moslems, some have been assimilated to Malay language and culture, while others maintain a separate linguistic and cultural identity, holding only their religion in common with other Malays. Moslems of this latter type are often inconsistently treated, being sometimes subsumed under the Malay category on religious grounds and sometimes considered as indigenous peoples on the basis of linguistic criteria. The Malays with whom the people of Padju Epat have the closest contact are the Bandjars, who make up about 80 percent of the population of the nearby province of South Kalimantan. There are several Bandjar families living in Padju Epat's villages of Telang and Siong, and the entire population of the village of Tampulangit is Bandjar Malay.

The remaining 45 percent of Borneo's population falls into a heterogeneous category, "Dayak," a term which is generally applied, following a Dutch convention, to all the non-Moslem indigenous ethnic groups of Borneo. In a more restricted British usage, not followed here, Dayak applies only to the Iban (Sea Dayak) and Land Dayak peoples of Sarawak. The term Dayak, then, has about the same specificity of meaning as the American word "Indian," and, like the latter, serves as a cover term for a heterogeneous assortment of named tribes.

Among the island's various Dayak tribes, groups of tribes can be isolated whose members exhibit a fair amount of cultural and linguistic homogeneity setting them apart from the members of other such groups. However, since no rigorous classification of Bornean tribes has ever been attempted, the number and constituency of such tribal groupings cannot be accurately determined at the present time. In general, Dayaks live in inland areas, dwell in relatively small, isolated communities, speak Malayic languages recognized as being indigenous to Borneo, and are animist or Christian in religion.

Traditionally, no Bornean groups called themselves Dayak, since the term is pejorative, meaning "hick" or "yokel." However, in the twentieth century, many of Borneo's ethnic groups have come to accept the name, adopting it to symbolize the solidarity of nationalistic feeling existing among Dayak tribes in opposition to "foreigners" such as the Chinese and Malays.

2

The Ma'anyan and the Padju Epaters

THE PEOPLE OF PADJU EPAT belong to a large Dayak tribe, called Ma'anyan, which numbers between thirty and thirty-five thousand people. The home territory of the Ma'anyan comprises the drainages of the Patai and Telang rivers, but during the late nineteenth and twentieth centuries, considerable numbers of Ma'anyan have emigrated northward into the less densely populated drainages of the Dayu, Paku, Karau, and Ayuh rivers.

In appearance, the Ma'anyan are much like other Indonesian peoples. Their stature is relatively short, their build slender, and their movements more graceful than those of the average Westerner. Skin color is generally light brown; hair, dark brown or black, and most often straight although some people have wavy or curly hair. Men normally wear Western style shirts with trousers or shorts, the traditional loincloth having been abandoned for many years. Women have adopted Malay dress, with its long batik skirt and long-sleeved blouse. Unmarried girls usually wear Western dresses. Headcloths and a variety of hats are worn for work in the fields, as protection from the scorching sun. Beautiful old cloths are reserved for ceremonial occasions, when a wealth of colorful finery emerges from household lofts.

The Ma'anyan have not always lived in the region they now occupy. Historical evidence seems to indicate that until the mid-seventeenth century, various Ma'anyan groups inhabited the fertile Hulu Sungai district in what is now part of the province of South Kalimantan. Their subsistence, then as now, was based on the cultivation of dry rice in swidden plots. To supplement their subsistence economy, the Ma'anyan grew pepper and gathered various forest products. These commodities found their way into the international market through Bandjar Malay traders who were based in the port towns of the south Bornean coast. Of these centers, Bandjarmasin came to be the most important. As the Dutch pepper monopoly gradually expanded over much of the Indonesian archipelago in the seventeenth century, the

Ma'anyan women in a moment of relaxation.

international demand for Bandjarese pepper increased to the point where it could no longer be met by the supplementary efforts of Dayak cultivators. As a result, non-Dayak farmers, mostly Bandjar immigrants and Javanese refugees from Mataram aggression, moved into the old Ma'anyan area as full time pepper cultivators. In the face of this incursion, the Ma'anyan retreated to the northwest to find new swidden territory.

Today the Ma'anyan tribe is divided into three named subgroups: the Benua Lima ("Five Villages") live to the south in the extreme eastern portion of Ma'anyan territory, the Padju Sapuluh ("Ten Villages") in the upper reaches of the Patai River, and the Padju Epat ("Four Villages"), in the Telang River drainage. The Ma'anyan themselves recognize this tribal subgrouping, which is made primarily along territorial lines, although each segment is also distinguished from the others by minor differences in customary law (*adat*) and by slight dialectal variations in language. At the same time, all Ma'anyan share a sense of common identity that sets them apart from contiguous ethnic groups such as the Lawangan Dayaks and the Bandjar Malays. Traditional histories maintained in the lore of each subgroup point to the common origin of all, while explaining the events that reputedly led to the development of the distinctive, though seemingly minor, differences separating them.

Traditional History

According to Padju Epat's own traditional history, all the Ma'anyan originated in a settlement called Sarunai, which was located some forty miles to the southeast of Padju Epat, near the present town of Amuntai in the province of South Kalimantan. One of the main cultural characteristics differentiating the Ma'anyan of that time from other Dayak groups was their practice of periodic mass cremation of the bones of their dead in a nine-day ceremony called *idjambe*. Each Ma'anyan settlement has a special cremation structure, called a *papuian*, that was the locus of the bone burning.

Sarunai was attacked and destroyed by people from a region called Tandjung Djawa. During the attack, many Ma'anyan were killed, their corpses beheaded, and the heads taken away by the raiders. According to Ma'anyan traditional law, a headless corpse could not receive *idjambe*, so two new types of death ceremony, not involving cremation, were devised for the victims of the raid. After the destruction of Sarunai, the Ma'anyan gradually withdrew to the northwest by several routes into the territories of the Patai, Telang, and Dayu river drainages. Several Ma'anyan villages still remain in the midst of Bandjar settlements in the Hulu Sungai area, vestiges of former Sarunai settlements.

In the exodus from Sarunai, the Ma'anyan broke up into the three subgroups known today. Under separate leaders, each settled in a different region, and each diverged from the others on minor points of customary law and dialect. The forefathers of the Padju Epat Ma'anyan established a small community on the banks of the Telang River, from which various new villages were settled as the population expanded.

Each new Ma'anyan village established its own cremation structure, transferring a bit of earth from the site of a previous *papuian*, and maintained its own ritual paraphernalia for the cremation ceremony. Then, according to the traditional account, a fanatic Islamic convert of Ma'anyan origin named Labai Lumiah, in a demonstration of zeal for his new religion, sought to Islamicize the Ma'anyan. As a first step, he set about eradicating all the *papuian* and paraphernalia for the *idjambe* ceremony. Being a Ma'anyan himself, he knew where each *papuian* was located and precisely what paraphernalia to destroy. Troops were apparently put at his disposal by the

Bandjarese sultan, for within a short time Labai Lumiah had swept through the Ma'anyan territories and had destroyed all the cremation structures but five in the villages of Padju Epat. Labai Lumiah approached Padju Epat from the east, but, in a pitched battle that is the glory of local tradition, was repulsed at Murutuwu by a combined force representing the five villages. The five *papuian* were saved.

In the other Ma'anyan villages which had been ravaged, no attempt was made to rebuild the demolished *papuian* or to replace the ritual apparatus required for the performance of the cremation ceremony. Padju Epat was thus the only Ma'anyan subgroup to maintain the custom of cremating the bones of its dead. The other groups made use of the death ceremonies that had been instituted for the headless dead of Sarunai following the Tandjung Djawa raid. Of course, this is a traditional account with a certain air of timelessness about it. Just when all this happened or was reputed to have happened, let alone whether it occurred only in part or not at all, is almost impossible to ascertain. However, the Padju Epat Ma'anyan burn the bones of their dead, and the other groups do not; the former refer to this tradition to account for the difference. Aside from its territorial identity, the custom of *idjambe* remains the most significant tangible characteristic setting off the Padju Epat segment from the other Ma'anyan groups.

Local traditions also account for the founding of each of Padju Epat's villages, following the retreat from their homeland of Sarunai under the leadership of a notable named Uriah Napulangit. The first settlement in Padju Epat was located on the south bank of the Telang River, near the present day village of Tampulangit. In the next generation, this village was abandoned, and a new settlement, called Halaman, was established farther upstream, reputedly by the grandson of Uriah Napulangit. The relatively poor soil around Halaman could support only a small population, and from time to time new settlements were established in the surrounding countryside. Of these, the villages of Siong and Murutuwu survive to the present day. Halaman was eventually abandoned as a village site, following a famous battle in which the Padju Epaters defeated a band of marauding Lawangan Dayaks from the north. The "Battle of Djuwung Salele," as the encounter is named, remains a popular Padju Epat tale of life in the olden days:

> In the days when Patinggi Walek was chief in the village of Halaman, there were two brave and famous warriors, Makulayu and Maku'ulai. The two, who were brothers, were renowned for their prowess in battle. One day, as all the other men were leaving the village to work in their fields, Patinggi Walek called the brothers to him, and charged them to stay in the village to guard it from attack.
>
> Unknown to Patinggi Walek, a fierce Lawangan leader named Marangau Pitau, with his ninety-nine followers, had concealed themselves in a spot where they could observe the village of Halaman. That morning, the marauders watched as Patinggi Walek and all the other men left the village for the fields. Once Halaman seemed unprotected, the Lawangans rushed in to destroy the village and capture its women and children. To their surprise, they were met by Makulayu and Maku'ulai. In the wild battle that ensued, the brothers slew all

ninety-nine Lawangan warriors. Only their leader, Marangau Pitau, managed to escape.

Marangau Pitau wandered aimlessly about the countryside, tired, thirsty, and very hungry. At last he came to a swidden house standing by itself in a rice field. He approached the house, and asked the man working on the porch for some food. The man, who was actually a cousin of Makulayu and Maku'ulai, said he could only spare a little cold rice. 'Cold rice,' in reality, was the title of his battle spear. As Marangau Pitau climbed the ladder up to the house, he received his 'cold rice,' and thereby met his demise.

When Patinggi Walek heard of the Lawangans' defeat, he was afraid that the spirits of their dead would vent their wrath on the people of Halaman. He decided that the village should be moved and set out to find a more propitious site. After wandering through the forest for some time, he came to a spring from which clear, fresh water bubbled. And this was the spot that he chose for his new village, which he named Telang, after the large thicket of bamboo (*telang*) which surrounded the spring.

The other Ma'anyan villages of Kararat and Balawa were founded from Telang, supposedly by two grandsons of the brave Maku'ulai. The one other village in Padju Epat, Tampulangit, is inhabited by Bandjar Malays and not Ma'anyan. As far as can be determined, this Bandjar enclave has existed for the better part of two centuries. The actual details of its origins have been lost in the passage of time, and there are three different traditional stories to account for its presence.

The first version explains that in pre-Dutch times, Padju Epat was under the suzerainty of the Bandjar sultan, who sent a contingent of Moslems to the area to assure its loyalty to the throne. A second account relates that the Padju Epaters themselves petitioned the sultan to send protection for their cremation ceremonies, the implication being that intruders would probably be Bandjars who could be best handled by other Bandjars. In the third story, the Padju Epaters are said to have requested that the sultan establish a resident Bandjar force in Padju Epat to protect the Ma'anyan from Lawangan raids. Each of these versions offers the corollary that, since Moslems would not be happy living in a Dayak village with its many pigs, the newcomers established their own village at a suitable distance from any Ma'anyan settlement. Whatever the truth of the matter, there has been a Bandjar settlement at Tampulangit for a long time, and its people maintain a close and harmonious relationship with Ma'anyan villagers, while remaining religiously and linguistically distinct from them.

The Land

What sort of land was inherited by the followers of Uriah Napulangit? In geographical perspective, the heartland of Padju Epat is dominated by a low, undulating line of hills that nowhere rise to a height of more than forty or fifty feet. In a number of the hollows formed between the hill crests, there are extensive marshes. The hills are cut by the Telang and Siong rivers together with their minuscule tributary trickles; it is on the banks of the larger waterways that the villages are located. The soil is poor, and the land area overspread with secondary forest, the only tree cover that remains after centuries of intensive swiddening. A Dutch visitor to the area over a century ago remarked even then on the absence of primary forest. The forest is spotted with the clearings of village sites, current and abandoned swidden plots, patches of savanna grass, and stretches of white sand, the latter representing the ultimate in soil degeneration. Here and there clumps of fruit trees, especially the giant durian, tower over the rest of the forest. Marking the locations of old swidden sites, these trees have sprouted from seeds tossed out by swidden farmers who had eaten the fruit. When a plot is recleared, the fruit trees are not felled, and as the years pass, the stand of trees becomes the living proof that an ancestor had farmed here.

Narrow paths linking swidden plot and village wind through the forest and traverse marshes on large felled tree trunks. Much wider trails, passable to bicycles, connect the villages with each other and Padju Epat with the outside world. Toward its outer perimeter, the hills flatten out as they approach the Barito River on the west and the Patai on the south. A low marshy area, called Banawa, separates Padju Epat from the adjacent Ma'anyan territory of Padju Sapuluh on the east.

The water flowing in the rivers of Padju Epat is characteristically brown in color with rather the appearance of tea; this hue is derived from the forest peat beds through which it has percolated as ground water. The upper courses of the Telang and Siong rivers are narrow, shallow, and overhung by brush. The streams flow southwestward in more or less parallel fashion, the former past the villages of Murutuwu and Telang, and the latter past Balawa, Kararat, and Siong, until they merge about a mile to the west of the village of Telang. The Telang River beyond this point flows almost due west in a wide, grassy bed that is within the flood zone of the Barito River. After passing the Bandjar village of Tampulangit, the rolling hills are left behind and the river flows through low, flat flood-forest over the rest of its length. About three miles below Tampulangit, at a spot called Muara Lotek, the main course of the river swings to the south-southwest and remains on that heading until it debouches into the Barito near the Bandjar town of Kelanis.

Between Tampulangit and the Barito, the Telang is navigable by sizeable motor boats throughout the year. During the dry season, the level of the river drops steadily. Between July and October, when precipitation is almost nonexistent, the river bed above Tampulangit is nearly dry, and no floating transport passes. However, between November and March, the heavy rains of the northwest monsoon cause the river to rise, its volume greatly augmented by the Barito's flood waters which back up as far as Telang. The flat, grassy plain through which the Telang River meanders between Telang and Tampulangit is flooded, making Telang accessible to large motor boats if the way has been kept clear from debris. High water at this time also permits small motorboats to reach the Telang directly from the Barito town of Bengkuang, a much shorter route than following the Telang River itself. Vast sections of low-lying forest between Tampulangit and the Barito are covered with water so that canoes, at least, are no longer restricted to the course of the river bed, but can be paddled deep into the woods over the submerged land.

Most of the low region between Tampulangit and the Barito is unsuitable for village sites because of this periodic flooding. However, there is a small Bandjar "floating hamlet" located at Muara Lotek, the confluence of the Telang and Pahalam rivers. The houses of this floating settlement are built on log booms. Its population derives the major part of its livelihood from fishing, although petty trade and a boat taxi service play some part in its economy. Most of the resident Bandjars have other homes in more permanent settlements like Telang Baru, Kelanis and Mengkatip.

Even small canoes are not generally used on the Telang and Siong rivers above their respective namesake villages: throughout the dry season, the water in their upper courses is too shallow for canoes; during the rains, the stream level is too high, and passage is obstructed by low overhanging branches and other impediments such as fish traps. If it is necessary to move an extremely heavy load along these upper courses, a small canoe can be fought along the stream with the expenditure of great effort.

The marshy areas that comprise Padju Epat's outer perimeter on three sides are flooded during the northern monsoon, and difficult to negotiate at other times. These marshes tend to isolate Padju Epat from the outside world, which has proved sometimes a boon and sometimes a curse. In the past, its geographical position has protected Padju Epat from undue external harassment, but in the present day the marshes present obstacles to the maintenance of good communications with the political and economic centers beyond its borders. Vehicular roads connecting Padju Epat with Tamiang Layang to the east and Dayu to the north were built under the Dutch at the end of the nineteenth and beginning of the twentieth centuries. Unfortunately, where they passed through the marshes, the roadbeds and bridges of these thoroughfares disintegrated during World War II under the Japanese occupation. To discourage Japanese inspections in the region, the Padju Epaters, finding it expedient to capitalize on their isolation, made no attempt to keep the roads open.

Paths for walking and bicycling are maintained along the course of the old roads, connecting Padju Epat with vehicular roads to the east. During the dry season, the twelve and a half miles to the nearby administrative center of Tamiang Layang can be covered in a little more than an hour by bicycle. The same journey may take four or five hours during the northern monsoon, when the clay path is treacherously slippery, makeshift bridges are inundated, and a good part of the path is under several feet of water.

3

The Village Settlement

FROM A DISTANCE, soaring coconut palms and fruit trees distinguish the site of a village from the surrounding forest cover. Each of Padju Epat's villages is located near the banks of a river, with its houses usually built above the normal flood zone. The stream serves as a bathing place for the villagers, although drinking water is often carried from clear water springs near the houses.

The village's residential nucleus consists of a group of wooden houses and other structures laid out on both sides of a broad sandy street. Scattered here and there along the street are clusters of coconut and areca palms, coffee bushes, and various flowering plants. Tall fruit trees provide shade, and cool groves of old rubber trees grow directly behind many of the houses. In appearance, the villages are neat and clean. Pigs and chickens, left loose to forage, effectively dispose of all garbage with dispatch. The village street is kept trim and free of grass by periodic work parties organized by the village head.

The Village House

Individual village houses (*lewu'*) are substantial wooden structures, built above the ground on ironwood piles. The longhouse, often considered the Dayak domicile *par excellence* in other parts of Borneo, is not found in the Ma'anyan region. Most houses are raised between three and six feet above the earth, but some of the oldest of the region's structures are elevated as much as fifteen to twenty feet. In the latter part of the nineteenth century, when occasional attacks from non-Ma'anyan Dayak groups to the north were still anticipated, houses were built high off the ground to make them more easily defensible and less vulnerable to surprise attack. The small number of highly elevated older houses that remain today were built in the 1880's and still reflect this defensive architectural feature. After the turn of the twentieth century, Padju Epat no longer feared such incursions, and the real need for high houses had passed. Houses built since that time are much lower, because it is an expensive and time-consuming task to acquire the supporting columns for a building. Short posts need not be as thick and heavy as the larger columns, and are easier for a few individuals to collect. Today, it is not only difficult to find timber suitable for the tallest piers, but it requires a considerable outlay of money and food to attract the laborers needed to transport and install the columns. Since the average number of nuclear families occupying each house has been declining over the last fifty years, and concomitantly the number of people to share the costs of putting in house posts has also been decreasing, newer houses tend to be built much closer to the ground than older ones.

Floors and walls are made of hand sawn planks and boards, for the nearest motor-powered saw mill is in Bandjarmasin. Most of the lumber used in Padju Epat is sawn locally, either in Tampulangit or in the nearest Bandjar towns on the Barito. Plank houses, however, are not traditional in the area, nor were they widely built until after 1910. Formerly village houses were built in the manner of large swidden houses, with sapling floors, bark walls, and palm-leaf thatched roofs. The first plank house was built in Telang by a resident missionary in the 1880's, and the second in the same village by the family of the district chief in 1899.

Roofs are usually in the form of a simple or truncated gable, airy with high ridgepole and good pitch to allow efficient run-off of rainwater. House roofs are covered by good quality, locally cut shingles, although a few newer houses are roofed with sheet tin. Each house has an ample supply of windows with shutters that can be opened wide during the day to admit light and fresh air, and then securely closed at night. There are two double-story buildings in Telang, both commercial structures resembling Chinese shophouses. Otherwise, all the houses in Padju Epat consist of but a single story. Padju Epat boasts a number of skilled, part-time carpenters, and its houses present a very trim appearance.

Kitchens are located in separate, less permanent structures attached to the side or back of the house, in order to lessen the danger from fire. The kitchen floor is raised on poles to the height of the house floor, and often there is an open porch as well. The walls are made of bark, and the roof is usually thatched with palm leaves. The floor is made of peeled saplings laid parallel to each other and lashed down with strands of rattan. Along one side of the kitchen at floor level there is a sand box which accommodates the wood fire. Baskets and metal cooking utensils hang on the walls, and enamel dishes for eating are stacked on shelves in the kitchen. Large jars, metal pails, and gourds for water storage stand along the wall. All food is prepared within the kitchen or on its open porch, the work being done in a squatting position. Garbage and unwanted food scraps are thrown through the floor's interstices to the ground, where they are consumed by foraging chickens, dogs, and pigs.

A village bathing place.

Specialized Structures

With the exception of Kararat, which consists of only two houses, each village has one or more specialized structures that are not used as habitations. Telang, Siong, Murutuwu, and Balawa each have a ceremonial hall known as the *balai*. The *balai* is occasionally used for the discussion of village disputes, but its primary function is connected with the *idjambe* cremation ceremony. The *balai* is square or rectangular in shape, with a heavy plank floor raised five or six feet above the ground on piles. Most *balai* have shingled roofs, but the one in Balawa has been covered with sheet tin as a mark of modernity. Various temporary porches and walkways are constructed on three sides of the permanent structure when a cremation ceremony is performed.

There is one smokehouse for curing rubber in Telang, one in Murutuwu, and two in Balawa. All of these are privately owned. One Siong resident has a smokehouse, but it is located about seven miles to the northwest of his village, near the town of Bengkuang; he owns a large rubber plantation there and can carry his smoked rubber out to the Barito by boat at all seasons of the year.

One or two houses in each village have small rice storage sheds built nearby. The normal practice, however, is for each family to keep the bulk of its unhusked rice in cylindrical bark storage containers in its swidden house, whence supplies can be carried periodically to the village as needed.

Schools and Education

Three of the villages, Telang, Balawa, and Murutuwu, have primary school buildings that house grades one through six. The Telang and Balawa schools are government operated, but Murutuwu's is a village-supported institution. Schools have been part of the Padju Epat scene for more than a century. The first, in Murutuwu, was established in 1851 by a German missionary but was later shifted to Telang when the mission was moved there in 1875. The Balawa school was built by the Dutch government in 1941. The Murutuwu school was opened in 1960, partly so that children would not have to walk seven miles each day to school, and partly because of a feud between Murutuwu parents and one of Telang's two teachers.

During some parts of the year the school buildings and their yards are thronged with boys and girls, but at other times the teachers have difficulty getting the children into the classroom. Although school-age children are required by Indonesian law to attend school, they form an important element in the village family's labor force. A few individuals try to keep their children away from school entirely so that they can be used full-time in the family's swidden fields. Other families, who do send their children to school, take them out of classes during the peak agricultural work periods such as planting and harvesting. During these seasons, Padju Epat's schools are generally closed, since the teachers, too, have fields to attend to.

Yet about 60 percent of all the people in the area have had at least one year of formal education, and about 77 percent are literate in Latin characters. Of the group that has received some schooling, the average is 4.3 years of education. Beyond the sixth grade, children must leave Padju Epat to take up residence in distant administrative centers where junior or senior high schools can be found. Usually this is possible only when a youth can live with relatives near a school. The nearest junior high school is located in Tamiang Layang, the district capital. Of Padju Epat's current inhabitants over fifteen years of age, about 7 percent had received some post-primary education. However, this figure understates the number of Padju Epaters who have received advanced education, for the region suffers from a brain drain. Few high school or even junior high graduates return to their home villages, a circumstance that gives parents mixed feelings about the value of an advanced education. Padju Epat can boast at least one absent son who has attained the doctorate as a veterinarian.

The New Center of Telang

Telang was traditionally the seat of Padju Epat's district chiefs, and it has continued as the region's administrative center under both the Dutch colonial regime and the current Indonesian government. In addition, it has been the site of Padju Epat's periodic market since the 1860's.

Around 1910, after the road connecting Padju Epat with towns to the east had been constructed, Bandjar Malay tradesmen began arriving to set up as shopkeepers in Telang's market area. However, these Moslems were reluctant to build houses in Telang's pig-infested village on the south side of the river, where the market area was located until 1930. The Bandjars were given permission to construct homes on the north side of the river, and a small community was established there about midway between the older settlements of Siong and Telang, but within the traditional territory of the latter. To avoid confusion, I call the settlement to the south of the river "Old Telang," and the newer one to the north, "Center Telang," although the villagers themselves do not make this distinction. In the late 1920's the bridge across the river became too weak to support vehicular traffic, and the site of the market was moved from Old Telang to Center Telang, where it is still located. After this shift, people other than Bandjars began to build houses in Center Telang. With the deterioration of its external road links during and after the Japanese occupation, Telang's market declined in importance and most of the Bandjar traders moved away, selling their Center Telang holdings to local people.

At the present time, Center Telang comprises ten or twelve houses, and a number of specialized structures reflecting its position as an administrative and economic center. There are two large open sheds that house itinerant traders on market day. There is a combination office and residence for the subdistrict officer. Across from the subdistrict officer's quarters stands the bare skeleton of a public health clinic upon which construction was started in March 1963, but which was never completed during my stay because the male public health nurse left the region and could not be replaced. The market sheds, the subdistrict officer's quarters and the clinic frame were all erected with the aid of cooperative labor contributed by the men of Padju Epat's villages.

A Christian church was raised near the market in 1964 by the congregations of Telang and Siong. Prior to that time, services in those two villages had been held in the homes of various members, a practice that continued to be followed in Balawa.

Center Telang has one more or less permanent coffee house, and there are four others that are open on market day or on other occasions apt to draw a crowd. There is also one permanent "notions" shop that dispenses matches, cigarettes, kerosene lantern wicks and chimneys, and a few other similar items. These buildings also serve as residences for their proprietors.

In 1964 each of Padju Epat's villages had some empty houses. The percentage and condition of the unoccupied structures varied somewhat among the different villages, however. For instance, in both Telang and Siong 36 percent of the houses were untenanted, while in Murutuwu, only 19 percent were vacant. In addition to this quantitative difference between Telang and Siong on the one hand and Murutuwu on the other, there was a qualitative one as well. Most of the vacant houses in the former two villages were decrepit and even uninhabitable, while all of those in Murutuwu were in good condition.

It must be noted that there are no vacant dwellings in Center Telang,

The village street in Center Telang.

and this settlement appears to be gradually absorbing the populations of both Old Telang and Siong. Almost no new buildings had been built in the latter settlements for a number of years. In Center Telang, at least six new houses had been constructed between 1961 and 1963 by both Telangers and Siongers, and several more were being planned when I left the area in 1964. The border separating the territories of Telang and Siong is located just fifteen yards to the northwest of the market area, which allows Siongers to settle in the Center Telang vicinity and maintain their traditional village territorial identity. It is quite possible that within the next ten to fifteen years the residents of Old Telang and Siong will have abandoned their old settlements and become consolidated into a single residential nucleus.

Ceremonial Components

In addition to its buildings, a Padju Epat village must contain certain ceremonial elements. These include village guardian statues, a cemetery, a cremation structure, and one or more elevated ironwood boxes in which the ash residue from cremation is deposited.

Two types of wooden statues serve as the homes of village guardian spirits. One type (*panungkulan*) guards the main land approach to the village; the other (*tungkup*) protects the approach by water and the village bathing place. The *panungkulan* is a tall wooden pillar, fifteen to twenty-five feet high, at the top of which a human figure with a gong on his head is carved. All of the statues stand at the entrance to the village, offering a threat to any advancing enemy; some brandish spears. Although these statues are erected by individuals, their spirits protect the land areas of the entire village from enemies. The river is protected by the wooden statue of a man (*tungkup*) placed in midstream. These statues, not as imposing as the *panungkulan*, rise only three or four feet above the surface of the water.

Each village has a cemetery (*si'at*) in which the remains of the dead are buried until their bones are exhumed for cremation. The Christian segment of Padju Epat's population prefers not to use the traditional burial areas; Telang, Siong, Balawa, and Murutuwu each have special Christian cemeteries, although the latter village no longer has any resident Christians.

In the forest near the village there is a cremation structure (*papuian*) raised on an earthen mound. The *papuian* is a small wooden frame on which the bones of the dead are burned on the ninth and final day of the big *idjambe* cremation ceremony. At the time of a ceremony, various temporary platforms, walls, and a roof made of light woods are added to the basic ironwood framework of the *papuian*. During the years intervening between cremation ceremonies, the temporary fixtures disintegrate, and the *papuian* is engulfed by fast-growing tropical vegetation.

A *tambak* is an elongated, richly carved ironwood box, five to seven feet in length and elevated four to five feet above the ground, that serves as a receptacle for the ashes of bones that have been burned during the *idjambe* cremation ceremony. A special area for *tambak* is located near the cremation structure in each village. In most villages the *tambak* area contains more than one *tambak*. Each *tambak* has its own name, and each is associated with a social group, the *tambak* group, to which individuals may gain membership by birth, marriage, or adoption. The ashes of a given *tambak* group's members are placed in its associated *tambak* after cremation. *Tambak* groups were traditionally ranked relative to one another in a stratified class system that no longer plays an important part in the organization of Padju Epat society. Within a village's *tambak* area, the various *tambak* have been placed in a line running parallel to the nearest river. The *tambak* are then arranged in the traditional rank order of their associated *tambak* groups, with those of higher status located upstream and those of lower status downstream. *Tambak* groups are perduring social units that usually maintain their existence over many generations. In the past, new *tambak* groups were occasionally established and old ones died out. Because of their ironwood composition, *tambak* are fairly long lasting. However, when one finally succumbs to the disintegrative forces engendered by the equatorial climate, it will be rebuilt, and will continue to be rebuilt as long as its associated *tambak* group endures. In 1963 there were twenty-two extant *tambak* in Padju Epat: eight in Telang, three in Siong, five in Murutuwu, one in Kararat, and five in Balawa.

From the brief summary given above, a picture emerges of the Padju Epat village as a row of houses laid out along a village street adjacent to a river. Each village, except Kararat, has a ceremonial hall and one or more special structures. Each village has a cemetery, a cremation structure, and one or more ash receptacles. The settlement is protected by guardian spirits who reside in wooden statues located at the main land and river entrances to the village.

Although its village settlement serves as the residential nucleus for each Padju Epat community, the permanent village house is usually occupied only intermittently. When I first moved into my house in Telang in April of 1963, the village seemed deserted. The street was empty except for a few stray chickens; windows were tightly shuttered. The elementary school was closed, and no children played in the street. Even toward dusk only a few houses showed signs of life. Soon I learned that the rice harvest was in full swing, and every family had moved to its swidden field until the new rice was in. Thus, in describing the Padju Epat village, I found it was also necessary to visit the swidden fields where villagers spend much of their time.

4

The Economic Sphere

Swidden Rice Cultivation

ALL THE MA'ANYAN OF PADJU EPAT and most of the Tampulangit Bandjars engage in swidden rice cultivation. There is no irrigated rice grown in Padju Epat. The agricultural calendar begins with the locating and clearing of new swiddens between May and July at the onset of the foehnal dry season that accompanies the southeast monsoon in the Padju Epat region. Brush and small trees in the new swidden are cleared first; then, usually with cooperative labor parties, the bigger trees are cut. When a large stand of trees is to be felled, it is done in series. A whole line of trees is boxed, though not chopped through completely. One tree at the head of the line is felled in such a way that it hits and topples the next tree, and so on down the row, like a line of towering dominoes. Between July and September, once the accumulated debris has become thoroughly dry, the new fields are burned over; larger logs and tree stumps remain in the blackened clearings.

Planting begins in October with the first light rains. With a long, pointed stick called a dibble stick, men punch shallow holes in the charred ground. Women and children follow behind, casting a few rice seeds into each hole, and eventually the entire field is sown. A small area of most fields is planted with fast maturing varieties of rice, including a special ceremonial glutinous type, that ripen in four months. The greatest amount of field space is devoted to species of rice that mature in six months, and from which a higher yield is anticipated. A field in its second or third year of consecutive use frequently is not planted with rice, but with cassava, sugar cane, bananas, pineapples, red peppers, eggplant, various squashes and gourds, a few leafy vegetables, and generally both betel and tobacco.

After the rice has begun to sprout, occasional weeding, an arduous job usually relegated to women, is required, especially in older fields. As the crop ripens, it must be carefully guarded to protect it from destruction by animals and birds. Harvesting begins in late February and continues through March and April, when the slower maturing species of rice are brought in. The harvester, who holds a small knife in the palm of his hand, cuts each stalk of grain and puts it into a basket tied at his waist. The stalks are then dumped onto a large mat spread on the ground, and the grain threshed with bare feet. Unhusked rice, which preserves well, is stored in bark containers. Much of the heavy work involved in clearing, planting, and harvesting is accomplished with the aid of cooperative work groups, which will be discussed in greater detail in a later chapter.

In each swidden plot a field hut (*dangau*) is built, either before or immediately after planting. To describe the *dangau* as a field hut does not do justice to some of the habitations so designated, for there is a great deal of variety in the size and sturdiness of individual structures. Some *dangau*, indeed, are quite small, with a floor area of only 10 to 15 square feet. Others are large, substantial structures with floor areas ranging up to 400 square feet. All, however, are built from the same materials, and all are raised above the ground on poles. The floors are made of stripped saplings, the walls of tree bark, and the roof thatched with palm leaves. Indeed, they look rather like large versions of the kitchens attached to village houses.

Some field huts are located up to 6 miles from the village; others as close as 100 yards. In Telang and Siong, for instance, the average *dangau* distance from the village is 1.43 miles, with a range of from 100 yards up to 6.3 miles. All the field houses lying more than a mile from the village are substantial structures, and so too are some lying closer to the village. Most families farm more than a single swidden plot, and the plots are often a considerable distance apart. The villagers feel that the possession of several plots lessens the chance of losing their entire crop if weather, bird, animal, or insect disaster should strike one field.

Although there are a few misanthropic individuals in every village who, for one reason or another, seek isolation in remote swiddens, the majority of the Padju Epaters are gregarious people who want company in their fields. Families who farm fairly close to the village often have no immediately contiguous neighbors, both because it is difficult to find extensive areas of suitable swidden land near the village, and because they can gratify their need for companionship by visiting either the village itself or other fields that are situated nearby.

An individual farming at any great distance from the village rarely makes much use of his village house, but returns only on special occasions. For him, the village house is like a hotel or town house, to be used when required. A nuclear family with school-age children will sometimes leave the children in the village house in the care of an older sibling or some other fairly permanent member of the larger household. Because of Telang's weekly market, the people of Telang and Siong probably make more use of their village houses than do members of other villages. However, when the market is at its lowest ebb from August to October, both Telang and Siong are practically deserted, and only a few families make daily use of their village houses. There are some individuals in every village who may not pass ten nights a year in the village.

The Swidden Hamlet

Individual nuclear families that farm more than two miles from their home village will find such an isolated situation acceptable only if the family is large enough to handle all the farming and crop guarding required, or if the family head likes to be alone. The decision to farm four or five miles from the village may be based on the availability of a plot of extremely fertile ground, or on the need to tap or guard rubber trees in the area. Since mature rubber trees can either be tapped or not without harm to the trees, a family may tap its trees at a distant location for a year or two, and then move closer to the village for a few years, as the spirit moves them. Most nuclear families that intend to farm at a great distance from the village try to find a few other families to join them in the area. Thus, in many parts of a village's territory, there are little clusters of swidden fields and *dangau* that form temporary hamlets the Ma'anyan call *bantai*.

A swidden hamlet is rather like a small, ephemeral village. The field houses are large and solid. If good land is plentiful nearby, and if the members of the constituent families do not get tired of each other, a hamlet may endure as a settlement for a number of years. Not all hamlets are far removed from the village; they may be found at close and intermediate distances as well. For example, four Siong nuclear families formed a hamlet only 1.1 miles from the village, while a Murutuwu hamlet of six field houses was only 1.2 miles distant. In the middle range, there was a Siong hamlet of three field houses located 2.8 miles from the village, and at the extreme, a six-hut hamlet situated 5 miles northwest of Siong.

Supplementary Subsistence Activities

In addition to the all-important field crops, a few other sorts of food may be added to the subsistence system. The rivers, especially between Telang and Tampulangit, yield a fair supply of fish, as well as an occasional turtle and small quantities of fresh-water shrimp. During the rainy season fish are taken piecemeal from the river in various types of traps and weirs. Some night fishing is carried on from canoes, using lanterns and spears. Occasionally a village will organize a fish-poisoning expedition, employing the poisonous *tuba* root (*Derris elliptica*). However, since the contaminating effects of this technique cannot be easily controlled, the party usually makes its way to some distant pool or stream within the village territory. Fresh fish is greatly prized, but much of what is taken from the river is salted and dried for use in lean times. As the dry season commences, fishing becomes progressively easier, up to a point, because the limits of the river gradually contract as the floodwaters recede, creating a greater fish density where water remains. However, eventually the stretch of river between Telang and Tampulangit gets so low that no more large fish can enter from the Barito. When the river reaches this level, fence-like dams are put up across the river at several points, and people from all over Padju Epat take part in a series of fish drives. The niceties are dispensed with, and the assembled throng of men, women, and children climbs into the shallow water; they probe the mucky river bottom with hands, nets, and spears to capture the fish that have buried themselves in the mud. The crowd drives down toward each dam in succession, catching boatloads of fish. But after a few days it is all over, and there is no more fishing in Padju Epat until the rains come once again.

At certain times of year, during their migration season, pigeons and parakeets are caught in the forest. High branches on fruit trees are smeared with tacky latex obtained from local rubber trees, and live decoys staked out to call their brethren to perch. When the bird lands, its feet become stuck fast to the branch. At this time one often sees a man returning to the village with fifteen or twenty cages on his back, each containing a colorful green and red bird. Pigeon is tasty, while parakeet has little to recommend it but its protein. During the height of the fruit season, groups of men and women go to the fruit groves at night to stretch large nets high in the trees. As giant fruit bats fly in to feed, they are snared in the nets. (Bat meat can be quite palatable when broiled or stewed.)

Considerable numbers of wild pig and various types of deer roam the forests, but these add little to the villagers' larder. In the days before firearms were widely distributed in the area, the blowpipe was a superlative weapon, and the skill of hunting with dog packs so highly developed that even the capture of a bear was not exceptional. However, for almost a century Padju Epaters have tailored their hunting techniques to the rifle and shotgun; there are only a few older men in the area who still, in a small way, maintain dogs for hunting purposes. Today, no one has any facility with the blowpipe, which is relegated to the status of an antique heirloom. At present, the weapon is used only in conjunction with a traditional style wedding ceremony which is rarely performed. As the groom approaches the house of the bride, he is supposed to shoot a dart over her house with a blowpipe to drive away any lurking, ill-intentioned spirits. At the one traditional wedding held during my stay in Padju Epat, the nineteen-year-old groom had to receive on-the-spot instruction from an old man on how to manipulate the blowpipe, and it was only after several attempts that a dart successfully completed its trajectory over the house. Thus has the art of the blowpipe passed.

At the present time, villagers are prohibited by law from keeping firearms, with the result that, having allowed their traditional hunting techniques to atrophy, they do not get much meat from the forest. A type of powerful bamboo spear trap is often hidden at strategic places near swidden fields and game trails. These traps are fatal to any animal unfortunate enough to hit the trigger line, and occasionally one blunders into such a trap to provide meat for the trap owner and his friends for a few days. Spear traps must be checked every day, for if this is neglected, the potentially lucky trapper may arrive to

Mud fishing during the dry season.

find an animal that is too badly decomposed to be eaten. Although quite useful for snaring wild pigs and deer, these traps can also inflict painful and often fatal wounds on unsuspecting humans who have not noticed the warning signals with which local tradition requires the marking of such traps. For this reason, the use of spear traps has been technically outlawed by government authorities.

It is, in fact, rather ironic that, with the decrease in the effectiveness of hunting activity, the forest animals, far from furnishing great amounts of food for the local populace, are jeopardizing the livelihood of the Padju Epaters. There has been an increase in the wild animal population which, on occasion, breaks into the cultivated fields, bringing much destruction to rice, fruit, and vegetables. The only defenses against such depredations are the fencing of entire swidden fields, an extremely laborious task, the erecting of scarecrow mechanisms, or continual patrolling of one's field.

Most families do keep a few domesticated pigs and chickens, but these are usually saved for ceremonial occasions, when large numbers of guests must be fed. Meat is thus a rare if much appreciated item in the local diet, and it is fish, fresh or dried, that provides the major source of protein for the Padju Epater.

A variety of fruits may be obtained in season. Bananas, pineapples, coconuts, planted by individual families in their swiddens or beside village houses, are available almost the year around. From December through March, various forest fruits ripen, including rambutan (*Nephelium lappaceum*), durian (*Durio zibethinus*), tjempedak (*Artocarpus champeden*), nangka (*Artocarpus integrifolia*), *langsat* (*Lansium domesticum*) and mangosteen (*Garcinia mango-stana*). During a good season, fruits are an important dietary supplement, and fruit gathering expeditions become occasions of great conviviality. Groups of young people often pass a gay evening joking and talking as they sit near an enormous durian tree waiting for its spiny fruits to drop. Not only are the trees too tall to climb safely, but the fruit is at its most succulent when eaten just after it has fallen. Many fruits are available in sufficient quantities to form an important export commodity from Padju Epat. Villagers gather fruits from their trees and sell them in the Telang market to Bandjar traders. Canoeloads of pungent ripe fruits from Padju Epat are eventually sold in Barito towns and in Bandjarmasin, one hundred miles downriver.

The Cash Economy

In addition to the sale of fruit, several other sources of cash income are open to the Padju Epat villager, the most important being an old and rapidly expanding rubber industry. The first rubber trees were planted in Telang over fifty years ago, and a few families still tap some of these. Since 1950 new trees have been planted in ever increasing numbers; in the last decade some 90,000 trees have been planted in Telang and Siong alone.

Rubber seeds are planted in a nursery plot with a dibble stick. Before transplanting, the young saplings are uprooted and trimmed to the semblance of a six-foot fishing pole, in which form they are carried in bundles to a second or third-year swidden plot and inserted into holes made with a dibble stick. During the first year after transplanting, the area around the trees must be kept clear of weeds, but since the swidden plot in which they grow is usually still being sown with rice or other crops, this weeding would be required in any case. In general, little work is necessary to maintain the rubber trees beyond the first year, and thereafter the trees are pretty much on their own, although some families pay more attention to their nascent rubber groves than do others. I have seen some unattended stands in which most of the trees had been ringed by nibbling deer. However, as with many other things, a certain amount of luck must attend the rubber trees that are to attain a productive maturity at about ten years of age.

In the early morning, the tapper makes a V-shaped cut near the base of a rubber tree, placing a coconut shell or other container at the point of the V to catch the sticky latex. In midmorning he collects the latex in a pail and brings it to a central collection point. The liquid is poured into a wooden box, a coagulant added, and once hardened, the thick bats of latex are dumped into open water holes, where they exude a strong and not altogether pleasant odor. Latex is usually sold in this form, although there are a few local smokehouses that produce a higher grade of smoke-cured sheet rubber.

In the wet season, rubber is sold directly to buyers who come to Telang by boat from the Barito towns. During the dry season, the movement of rubber is difficult: some is arduously transported to Tamiang Layang by bicycle;

some is bought up by local entrepreneurs, muscled out over the muddy river bed to Tampulangit and thence to the Barito by canoe; some is saved until the onset of the rainy season, especially in families where cash is not needed immediately.

Rubber trees require only a small investment in money and time, and offer an economic resource that need be exploited only when, where, and to the extent that each individual family sees fit. Its cultivation fits comfortably into Padju Epat's swidden-based but diversified economic complex, providing a useful source of supplementary cash income without forcing an overcommitment to a particular form of economic specialization. Rubber cultivation has become so important to the Padju Epat economy that almost every nuclear family plants some rubber every year.

Indeed, the planting pattern seems to be so well established, that some Padju Epaters are beginning to express the fear that decent swidden land, or such as exists in the area, may become impossible to find within a few years. It is difficult to discount local expert opinion on such a matter, but such an outlook may be overly pessimistic. It is the usual practice in Padju Epat to plant rubber trees in rows about 3 yards apart, giving an average tree density of about 440 per acre. Telangers and Siongers between them are planting some 11,000 new rubber trees every year. If the planting process were maintained at the present rate, this would fill only 1.96 square miles or 2.7 percent of their combined areas in fifty years. At the end of the fifty-year period, old trees would be nearly ready to be culled, and no new area would be required.

Therefore, even if one correctly assumes that much of the territory of Telang and Siong is uncultivable, fears that rubber trees will soon usurp all productive swidden land seem unfounded. All this assumes, however, that the inhabitants of Padju Epat will continue to consider swidden cultivation as the major activity upon which their economy is built. Rubber is seen as only one source, though a major one, of supplemental income, and this helps to offset the deleterious effects of declining swidden production. Most villagers feel that the rubber market is a chancy thing. World demand varies, and prices fluctuate. No one wants to be totally dependent on factors over which he has no control. Thus, unless the total Padju Epat economic pattern changes, an occurrence that would require major psychological readjustments by its inhabitants, rubber cultivation will continue in the foreseeable future as an activity ancillary to swidden farming.

Young men may gain income by cutting trees in the low-lying forests to the west of Tampulangit and, when the area is flooded, floating logs out to the Barito for ultimate sale in Bandjarmasin. Rattan, which grows as a thick, thorny vine, is also gathered from the marshy areas between Telang and Tampulangit for sale on the Barito. Cutting rattan for commercial use is an arduous task not much to the liking of the Padju Epaters, although Bandjars from Tampulangit and Barito towns occasionally supplement their income in this manner. Considerable quantities of rattan are used by the villagers themselves for everything from tying up bundles to weaving carrying baskets and floormats; the bitter core of the vine also serves as a vegetable.

Padju Epat is known for its production of dugout canoes, which are sold along the Barito for supplemental income. This industry was extensive even in the last century, when it was described by a touring Dutch civil administrator in 1857:

> The work of the Padju Epaters focuses principally on rice agriculture, with the manufacture of canoes next in importance. All the canoes that are used on the Barito and in the sultanate are made almost exclusively by the Dayaks of Padju Epat. Hundreds and hundreds of them are brought down the river by them every year in order to be sold. These canoes are chopped out of a tree trunk and the sides are then bent outward, over a fire, to the required shape. Through their industry, the canoe makers have denuded the whole territory of heavy timber so that at the present time it is only by renting forest tracts from their neighbors that they are able to continue their profession.

It would appear that the lack of primary forest in Padju Epat is not entirely due to over-swiddening. Canoe-making is not quite the industry that it was in the 1850's, but it is still an important potential source of cash income for some individuals.

Several small cafes, selling coffee, tea, and various snacks like fried bananas, are maintained in Telang. Others are opened and closed periodically in the other villages, depending on the potential for business at any given time. During June and July 1963 when the cremation ceremony was held consecutively in Murutuwu, Siong, and Balawa, large crowds gathered on each occasion. As the ceremony got under way in each village, a number of stalls were set up by local and outside entrepreneurs to dispense refreshments at a tidy profit.

The Periodic Market

Padju Epat supports a market which is held every Tuesday in Telang where a special area and a shed are set aside for that purpose. It should be mentioned in passing that Padju Epat has had a market for well over a century, although how much older the institution is cannot be determined. In the 1850's, the area's market was held twice weekly in Murutuwu, with all transactions by barter and rice as the principal medium of exchange. In the 1860's, the locus of the market was moved to Telang when that village became the administrative center for Padju Epat.

Telang's market is part of a periodic market system, in which a market is held each day of the week in a specific town. Telang, lying at the edge of the Barito River system and at the westernmost outpost of the old Dutch road network, participates in two regional periodic market systems. The first involves market relations with towns in the Patai, Dayu, and Paku-Karau river drainages, in which all the towns and villages are joined by land links. All but Telang currently lie on a vehicular road, which runs from Kelua in the adjoining province of South Kalimantan (whence it runs southward to the port city of Bandjarmasin) to Dja'ar (with a Sunday market), Tamiang Layang (Monday), Dayu (Wednesday), Tampa (Thursday), Ampah (Friday), and back to Patung (Saturday). Broad trails running along the beds of the former road connect Telang and its Tuesday market with Tamiang Layang to the east and Dayu to the north. The second regional market system links Telang by water with the Barito towns, although only Bengkuang (Wednesday) and Buntok (Friday) seem to have regular weekly markets. Most of the other Barito towns in the area deal with large trading boats that ply up and down the river between the port city of Bandjarmasin and Muara Tewe, some two hundred miles to the north.

All market transactions are based on money, either cash or credit. During my stay in Padju Epat the price of goods coming from or destined for the outside steadily increased in response to the general Indonesian inflation experienced in 1963 and 1964. However, commodities that stayed within the local area did not seem much affected by price fluctuations.

The market, like everything else in Padju Epat, experiences great seasonal variations. During the rainy season, when the water link with the Barito is open, the Telang market is a thriving affair. Kerosene, tobacco, cloth, sugar, pots and pans, medicines, and other necessary commodities as well as various luxury items, are brought in from the Barito by boat, since the trail from Tamiang Layang is generally in too poor condition to permit easy passage of heavy loads. However, a few hardy traders who specialize in lightweight items such as jewelry, plastic knick-knacks, and children's confections, come in from Tamiang Layang by bicycle for Telang's Tuesday market and then move on to Dayu the next day. A hard life, this. During the rainy season, Padju Epat does a thriving export trade in fruit, rubber, and canoes on market days, and at the height of the fruit season, there is a special market held every day in order to get the abundant crop to the external markets while it is still fresh.

Local trade is also transacted in the market. Women from all the villages of Padju Epat bring their vegetables, spices, coconuts, cassava, and sugarcane to a special section of the market area and there dispose themselves on the ground in a long line with their wares placed in front of them. People with fish to sell lay them out in a line opposite the vegetable ladies. During the "bird season" colorful pigeons and parakeets can be bought for the larder, and, infrequently, the meat of a wild animal is placed on sale. This is a rather rare occurrence, however, since the meat of wild animals is usually not sold, but portioned out among relatives, neighbors, and friends. Everyone has a fine time on these big market days, selling a little, gossiping, buying, or bargaining for the fun of it, and sipping coffee in the cafes.

With the onset of the dry season, the markets gradually decline; as the depth of the water decreases, larger boats can no longer navigate to and from Telang. By July, motorboats, with the large assortment of goods that they carry, can no longer reach the village. After the fruit season is over, only bananas can be bought regularly. Vegetable gardens do not receive sufficient rainwater, and the market supply dwindles. Fish, especially the larger kinds, are no longer brought to sell, but are kept for personal consumption. A few

Telang's market at the height of the fruit season.

bicycle traders continue to come to Telang into August, but by September the market seems moribund, not to be revived until high water returns with the rains of the northern monsoon.

5

Religious Groups in Padju Epat

T RADITIONALLY THE LIVES OF PADJU EPAT VILLAGERS were regulated by a customary legal code (*adat*) that was an integral part of the system of beliefs that underlie the local animist religion, known as Kaharinganism. However, at the present time, two nontraditional religions are represented among Padju Epat's population: Islam, which claims 3 percent of the people, and Christianity, with 19 percent. Although there are a few Moslems residing in Telang (21) and Siong (4), and a fair number of Christians in Telang (48), Siong (30), and Balawa (77), in 1963 the majority of Padju Epat's population (78 percent) was still to be counted as *Kaharingan.*

Kaharinganism or Animism

Kaharingan is the general term applied to the animist religions of the Barito area, and is not limited to the Ma'anyan in its use. Although the details of belief may vary from one ethnic group to another, in the *Kaharingan* world each living thing is animated by a life force peculiar to itself. Even inanimate objects may house spirits. The world at large is populated by spirits, some benign, some malevolent. The *Kaharingan* Dayak has developed a series of rituals to help him maintain an harmonious relationship with the spirits of his ancestors, and of the trees, plants, and animals around him upon which he is dependent. These rituals include spirit-propitation and village welfare ceremonies, agricultural ceremonies, curing ceremonies, and life-cycle ceremonies, the most important of which is the elaborate cycle of death ritual culminating in cremation.

Despite the vast array of particular rituals performed to celebrate every aspect of life, most Padju Epat ceremonies hold many elements in common. Special offerings of food, such as rice steamed in bamboo tubes, are prepared for the spirits, and plaited decorations are fashioned from palm leaves. Offerings and ritual equipment, including large gongs and old Chinese plates, are piled on the floor. Men and women sit on the floor, talking among themselves; children wander about, and babies sleep in their mothers' arms. A few old women chant softly, offering the spirits food. In most ceremonies the host family must feed an assembly of guests, and depending upon the importance of the event, chickens, a pig, goat, or water buffalo is killed to provide a meal for all. Large ceremonies are great social occasions, where the unmarried young gather to joke and tease, and the women can gossip freely. A gambling game often begins in a quiet spot, where the men collect, and at the big cremation ceremony, cockfights attract throngs of spectators, who bet on the outcome of the match.

Although certain minor rituals can be performed by any knowledgeable adult, most ceremonies require the services of a religious specialist, the shaman (*wadian*), for their proper accomplishment. There are seven different types of shaman, six relegated to women and one to men. Each has its own characteristic spirits, rituals, and functions. Padju Epat has a fair number of practicing shamans, who comprise from 7 to 9 percent of its population. The shaman must be able to go into trance, for trance is the door to the spirit world where, especially in healing ceremonies, the causes and cures for sickness must be sought. She must be an expert dancer, must possess the stamina to see her through a ritual that may last between an hour and nine days, and above all she must be able to master verbatim the countless chants which accompany the ceremonies she will be called upon to perform. In addition to her function as a religious practitioner and healer, the shaman also fills the role of local historian. Among her chants is a complete recounting of the origins and wanderings of the Ma'anyan people, the whys and wherefores of their customs and traditions, the names of their heroes, and the genealogies of their great families. Finally the shaman provides the village with its primary source of entertainment. All performances are "open to the public," and it is a quiet week when there is no shaman ceremony in at least one of the villages of Padju Epat. Padju Epaters, regardless of religion, will travel miles to watch a famous shaman in action.

Most of the population consider Kaharinganism to be a religion on a par with Christianity or Islam, and feel that the only reason that it is not accepted officially as such by the Indonesian government is because there is no *Kaharingan* "book" comparable to the Koran or the Bible. As a *Kaharingan*, a Dayak must maintain an elaborate and expensive system of rituals. If he wishes to divest himself of this ceremonial burden, he cannot just stop giving ceremonies, but feels that he must convert to another religion. In voluntary conversions, few Ma'anyan choose Islam. It is not clear whether this is because of a long-time cultural antipathy built up against Islam through former conflicts with its Bandjar Malay representatives, or because of a disinclination to adopt certain Islamic customs such as refraining from the consumption of pork. What does seem evident, at least in Padju Epat, is that *Kaharingan* are converted to Islam only through marriage. Such marriages as do occur seem to involve a *Kaharingan* woman and a Moslem man, for I have no records of a *Kaharingan* man marrying a Moslem woman.

Shamans chanting during the nine-day cremation ceremony.

Islam

Excluding Tampulangit, Padju Epat's Moslem population was concentrated in Telang. Sixteen of Telang's twenty-one Moslems were represented by an old Bandjar man of Tampulangit origin, his two wives who lived in separate households, and his descendants. This man had moved from Tampulangit around 1917 to set up shop in Telang's market area during its palmy days. He built a large house in the Center Telang area and stayed on after World War II when other Moslem traders of more distant origins had moved away. A young Bandjar, his wife, and three children made up the final segment of Telang's Moslem population. A native of Kelanis on the Barito, this young man worked as the subdistrict officer's assistant, a government post that had been proffered him as a discharged Army veteran. Siong's four Moslems formed a single family, including a Tampulangit man, his Siong wife, and their two children. As is customary in such marriages, the wife converted to Islam even though the couple decided to settle in Siong, where more agricultural land was available than in Tampulangit.

Padju Epat's Moslems do not participate in Islamic religious activities to any great extent. Before the Japanese occupation there was a small village mosque in Center Telang. Today, however, the nearest mosque is located down the river in Tampulangit. It is attended irregularly, and then only by the male heads of Padju Epat's Moslem families. There is no apparent adherence to a system of daily prayer or to the other requirements in the pillars of Islamic faith, although token fasting is observed at the beginning and end of Ramadan, and major holy days are celebrated with readings from the Koran and small ceremonies within the Islamic households.

Christianity

Despite early Protestant mission activity in the area, Christianity's roots are not very deep in Padju Epat. With a few exceptions, most of the individuals baptized in the nineteenth century were Kapuas Dayaks from the area to the west of the Barito, some of whom had been bought as slaves by the early missionaries and then freed. Two Telangers were baptized around 1911 and another in 1921. One or two Padju Epaters were converted to Christianity while living outside the area, but there was very little activity between 1921 and 1939. Since then, the pace of conversion has accelerated somewhat, partly because it is considered a progressive thing to do, and, increasingly at the present time, to seek relief from the economic burdens of animist ceremonial requirements.

A number of Padju Epaters claim they will convert as soon as the "old folks" have died and been cremated. Others are baptized and then revert to Kaharinganism under family pressures. Even death has not always brought an end to religious indecision. One old woman of Telang origin had spent much of her life as an emigre in Buntok to the north, where she became a Christian. After her death in 1951, she was buried in Buntok's Christian cemetery. Shortly thereafter, her remains were disinterred by her *Kaharingan* son and carried to Telang for the 1951 cremation ceremony. Telang's Christian leaders were alerted to the situation by their Buntok confreres and prevented the burning of the lady's bones. She now lies peacefully, at long last, in Telang's Christian cemetery. There was talk of mass conversion in Murutuwu after the completion of its 1963 cremation ceremony, but at the time of my departure in the spring of 1964, nothing had come of it.

Today the Kalimantan Evangelical Church, to which Padju Epat's congregation belongs, is entirely in Dayak hands. Foreign missionaries play almost no part in pastoral affairs, but are limited to a few specialized positions, such as teaching in the Church's theological seminary in Bandjarmasin. Padju Epat's Christian community gets along without the services of a resident minister. The nearest ordained minister of the Kalimantan Evangelical Church lives in Tamiang Layang. He comes to Padju Epat two or three times a year, at which times he performs baptisms, confirmations, and, occasionally, weddings. However, the day-to-day religious affairs of the Christian community are governed by the elders of the local congregation.

The Christians of Telang and Siong meet jointly in prayer services twice weekly. Until the spring of 1964, services were held in the houses of the members of the Christian community. However, since the completion of the church in Center Telang in March 1964, services are now regularly held there. The Christians of Balawa hold their own separate services and do not participate in those of the Telang–Siong congregation. Special services are held at Christmas, Palm Sunday, and Easter, and services were held every night during International Prayer Week in 1963. The services are usually led by members of the congregation. A text is read, generally from an Indonesian translation of the Bible, and this is followed by extended commentary in Ma'anyan by one of the Christian elders with occasional observations by other members of the assembled group. The service is interspersed with hymns. In keeping with Ma'anyan ceremonial tradition, a little food is usually served after each service. Occasionally the congregation would meet at the house of a sick member, which seemed, in a way, to be substituting for a shaman's curing ceremony.

Relations between Religious Groups

As a general rule the people of the different religious groups get on well together. They attend each other's ceremonies as observers if not as participants. One interesting feature of participation by the Moslems in Christian or *Kaharingan* ceremonies involves the slaughter of sacrificial animals (other than pig) and the preparation of food. When Moslem attendance is anticipated at a Christian or *Kaharingan* ceremony, chickens are killed according to Islamic tenets, and Moslems are invited to do the actual cooking. During the cremation ceremony, the sacrificial water buffalo is first stabbed with spears in traditional *Kaharingan* fashion, but as the animal falls, a Moslem rushes forward to slit its throat, thereby making the meat acceptable to all. Given the lack of sophisticated entertainments in the area, *Kaharingan* shaman ceremonies are a great attraction, attended by members of all three religious groups.

Generally members of a single household belong to the same religion. However, there are a few exceptions, and this often leads to friction among individuals within the affected household, because of ceremonial conflicts. In a few cases, this has led constituent nuclear families within such a bi-religious household to withdraw and set up new, independent households. Where a marriage involving individuals of different religions has occurred, the animist member has usually converted to the religion of his Christian or Islamic spouse. There were no current cases in Padju Epat involving a Christian–Moslem marriage.

There is a generally asymmetrical character to interreligious conversion in Padju Epat. The only mode of recruitment of Kaharinganism is by birth; to Islam by birth and marriage; to Christianity by birth, marriage, and self-conversion.

6

The Concept of Adat

ADAT, IN ITS GENERAL SENSE, means "custom" or "tradition"; it is also used in a narrower sense to convey the concept of "customary law." For the people of Padju Epat, it carries both meanings. If you ask why a woman wears her headcloth in a particular way, you are told, "It's *adat*. It's the traditional way. We've always worn it like that." And that is as much of an explanation as you will get, although you are apt to collect a lot of unsolicited information about the way in which the women of other ethnic groups wear their headcloths. In the same manner, if you ask why a particular individual, after burning his swidden field, kills a chicken, collects some of its blood on three plates, and then distributes money in the amount of 75 *rupiah* among a group of onlookers, you are also told it is according to *adat*. However, if you press your inquiry further in this case, you will be informed, "Well, he accidentally scorched some fruit trees while he was burning his field, and a chicken, three plates, and 75 *rupiah* was the ritual fine assessed to placate the spirits of those trees." Further questioning will elicit a whole scale of fines which might apply in a similar situation, depending on the number, size, and ownership of the trees, and whether the burning was intentional or accidental. The *adat* in this second case is part of a complex oral traditional code which can be referred to more specifically as *adat* law.

The body of *adat* law contains an extensive list of provisions specifying the fines or other forms of redress required to rectify any and all social infractions of a ritual, civil, or criminal nature. Have you opened a swidden out of season or across a public thoroughfare? Have you burned a *tambak*? Have you murdered someone or eloped? Have you married your daughter? The *adat* legal code covers all these contingencies and many others necessary to put the offending individual and the community back into a state of ritual and social balance.

However, the *adat* legal code provides for more than restitution. It also contains a schedule of ritual payments that should be made at the time of various life crises, such as a naming ceremony or a marriage, to placate any malevolent spirits that might be hovering about, and to offer public testimony to the fact that the event had been carried out in an approved fashion.

In the light of these two, rather different *adat* legal functions, we can divide Padju Epat *adat* legal provisions into two categories, one fitting into a system of "restitutive" *adat* law and the other into a system of "testimonial" *adat* law.

Adat Fines

All fines consist of two parts: the payment of an amount of money and the slaughter of one or more animals. In pre-Dutch times the valuables in the area were Chinese porcelain plates, and the fines mentioned in the *adat* legal code are frequently expressed in terms of numbers of plates. Originally perhaps plates changed hands with the payment of fines, but with the coming of the Dutch, silver coinage was substituted for plates according to a fixed schedule of value equivalents. Thus one plate was worth 25 cents; four plates, 1 *rupiah*; and eight plates, 2 *rupiah*. The introduction of paper money after independence has upset the scale of equivalent values. In this situation an adjustment factor is applied to establish how many paper *rupiah* are equivalent to a former silver *rupiah*. During my stay in Padju Epat, with the price of a pack of cigarettes at around 50 *rupiah*, the adjustment factor was ten to one. Thus a fine of eight plates or 2 silver *rupiah* could be paid with 20 paper *rupiah*. Such a fine was not considered to have much force in deterring breaches of the *adat* code. Even though the actual fines are paid in paper money now, the proper number of plates must be produced and stacked on the floor when a fine has been assessed.

The killing of a chicken suffices for fines of eight plates and under, but anything higher requires the slaughter of at least one pig to fulfill the payment of the fine. One or two special ceremonies require the killing of a goat and, in the case of the *idjambe* cremation ceremony, the slaughter of a water buffalo.

This brings us to one of the fundamental elements in all Padju Epat *adat* ceremonies, *pilah*. When an *adat* regulation has been broken, not only does the social harmony of the community become unsettled, but, more important in the ritual sense, the delicately balanced relationship between the spirit and human worlds is disturbed. This imbalance offers a ritual threat to the whole community, not just to individuals. In cases of extreme imbalance, such as murder, incest, and illegitimate birth, if the case is not properly adjudicated, it is thought that trees will not bear fruit and rice in the fields will not ripen. The balance is not fully restored until a ritual fine has been properly assessed and paid, and the people or objects actively or passively involved in the transgression have been spattered with blood from a freshly slaughtered animal. This spattering of blood, which is usually applied with a frond of leaves, is termed *pilah*. *Pilah* serves both to purify and to give ritual protection to the manifold objects or persons to which it is applied. It is used in all life-cycle ceremonies, at ceremonies attending the commencement of something new, such as the building of a house, and is applied also at the end of all *adat* legal cases to validate the decision reached. The blood used in *pilah* comes from the animal used in paying the *adat* fine.

The Adjudication Process

A closer look at the actual workings of the *adat* legal system reveals, first of all, that the Padju Epat *adat* legal code is not written down anywhere, but is maintained solely in the minds of individuals. Some people gain a greater mastery over the complex corpus of *adat* law than do others, a mastery attributable to various proportions of natural ability, determined memorization, and practical experience in handling actual legal cases, both restitutive and testimonial. Because of differences in degrees of expertise, and because of slight variations in the *adat* codes of each of Padju Epat's villages, not everyone has precisely the same conception as to the specifics of the law. This is one source of flexibility in the system.

Secondly, *adat* cases are decided not by individuals, but by groups composed of acknowledged *adat* experts sitting as a group. These *adat* experts, or adjudicating elders, are termed *mantir*. Each village has a small number of these elders who are known and respected as knowledgeable in *adat* matters. In each village there is also a chief officer in *adat* affairs, the *pangulu*, who is usually the foremost *adat* expert in the community. He serves as the senior *mantir*. When a problem of *adat* law arises, these elders will be invited to consider the matter. First, one or two elders will be consulted for advice. If it is a simple matter, and no animus between litigants is involved, the problem can be resolved without further ado. Especially in testimonial cases, an appropriate "fine" or sacrifice will be suggested by the elder or elders present, which will then be accomplished by the appellant. This is merely a matter of seeking expert advice, as we might do in drawing up a will; the individual is free to seek such advice or not. Such a procedure would probably be followed in the case of the scorched fruit trees mentioned above.

However, in a serious restitutive case where the welfare of a large group of people is involved, or where there are contending litigants, a different procedure is followed. The *adat* head and a group of elders will be invited to consider the matter. There is no set number of elders who must be present, and often elders will be invited from other villages. However, an elder who is invited is not obliged to attend the hearing of the case. The interest of the elders in sitting on a particular case may be directly proportional to the potential severity of the fines involved, for the slaughtering of one or more animals is part of the fine, and the elders are fed on the meat of the animals killed. Minor fines may involve only a chicken or two, whereas one or more pigs may be assessed in serious cases. The prospect of a pork dinner gives added incentive to the elders to show up for important cases.

When the *adat* head and elders have been convened, the facts of the case are put to them by the appellant or litigants. The task is then laid upon the assembled elders to decide who, if anyone, is at fault, and what the fines should be. In reaching their decision, the elders must give consideration to the two basic principles of the *adat* adjudication process, precedent and equity. Having satisfied themselves as to the facts of the case by extensive questioning, they determine what, if any, precedents are involved. The relevant articles in the *adat* legal code are then recited, together with their associated schedule of fines. This leads to a discussion of the particularistic aspects of the case at hand and the presence or absence of any mitigating circumstances. For the Padju Epaters are more interested in the spirit than the letter of the law. With this groundwork out of the way, the elders then review any cases known to them which have similar characteristics, a process that often takes a long time, because not everyone present may be familiar with or agree on the details of some of the precedents. Finally the individual elders begin to express their own opinions about the disposition of the case under consideration. There may be considerable disagreement at this juncture as to which article of the legal code to invoke, which litigant is at fault, and what fine should be levied. During most of the preceding deliberations, the *adat* head has remained silent unless called upon to render an opinion on some point of law or precedent. When it appears that the assembled elders have completed the presentation of all relevant arguments and are slipping into repetitious expositions of their respective points of view, the *adat* head quietly intervenes to sum up the various salient points and give his own opinion. Usually the other elders will concur with his judgment not only because they respect his legal acumen, but also because the prerequisites for the position of *adat* head are both unlimited patience and skillful persuasiveness. Naturally, individual men differ in the enactment of this role. Of the three that I saw in action, two *adat* heads could best be described as consensus spokesmen. The third was a consensus maker.

If the elders come to an agreement through the process described above, the judgment is announced and the fine stipulated. The animals required in the fine are killed and cooked on the spot while the elders conclude the ritual part of their duty. Blood from the killed animals is collected in a plate, and each elder dips a finger into the blood, rubbing it on his foot to signify his agreement with the legal decision just completed. Anyone or thing connected with the case requiring cleansing is sprinkled with some of the blood. The monetary portion of the fine is collected and placed next to the plates representing the assessed fine. Some of the money is then redistributed amongst the elders, serving partially as a fee and partially as witness money. In a case requiring the killing of a pig, the *adat* head and perhaps a senior elder will receive a portion of the slain animal. Their business concluded, the elders swap stories or compare notes on *adat* until the food is ready; the consumption of the meal brings the case to an end.

If the elders are unable to come to an agreement on the verdict, then the case is suspended and should be taken before a higher authority, the district *adat* head (*damang*) for his consideration. Here, theoretically, the whole procedure is repeated, with the *damang* sitting as head elder. If the elders agree

Adjudicating elders hearing an adat *legal case.*

on a verdict, but an appellant found to be in the wrong refuses to accept the verdict, two courses of action are open. The case can be referred to the district *adat* head if the elders feel that the disputant has a reasonably legitimate legal argument for not submitting to the judgment against him. However, if the disputant is felt to be clearly in the wrong, the elders have the power to eject him from the *adat* community. The individual who is "put outside *adat*" is not physically banished from the community. What is more serious, he is removed from the protection of *adat* law. Theoretically, a person placed outside *adat* can have any harm worked against him, including murder, and no notice would be taken by the *adat* legal system. This would happen only if the individual had some bad enemies and no relatives willing to protect him, and no cases of such dire retribution are known to have occurred in Padju Epat within recent memory. In the more usual case, the person put outside *adat* is sent to social and ritual Coventry. On the social side, no one in the community will help him to clear, plant, guard, or harvest his fields or assist him in any other type of cooperative activity. In the ritual sphere, no shamans will serve him, and no one will help him celebrate the various life crisis ceremonies required by his immediate family. This is strong medicine indeed for a true *Kaharingan*. I recorded one case in which a Sionger, found guilty in *adat* court of a serious offense, refused to accept the elders' judgment, and was put outside *adat*. This individual, one of the true misanthropes in the area, farmed with his wife and children in an isolated swidden several miles from the village. He was stubborn and seemed to be making out all right, when suddenly one of his children died. No one would help him to prepare the corpse, and the body was refused burial in Siong's cemetery. In the face of this calamity, the recalcitrant finally gave in, paid the fine, and was reinstated into the *adat* community. The threat of being excluded from the *adat* community is a strong negative sanction indeed.

In spite of the lengthy list of fairly explicit provisions contained in the legal code, the legal system maintains a healthy degree of flexibility. Because it remains unwritten, old articles that have not been invoked for a generation or two tend to drop out of the general public's cognizance, although they may remain longer, encrusted in the minds of a few experts with exceptional memories. When new situations arise that have no precedents in the system, the assembled elders establish a settlement on the basis of reason and equity, and this decision is then incorporated into the code as precedent for future reference.

Most Padju Epaters take a lively interest in *adat* matters. Since all *adat* hearings are open to the public, most people have witnessed any number of cases, both in the restitutive and testimonial systems. Their interest in things *adat* is not restricted to the narrow realm of Padju Epat. They are born comparativists, and since most people in the district have spent at least some time living up-country in close proximity to members of other Dayak groups, all can recount interesting if somewhat disjointed little tidbits of *adat* law related to these groups. When I first arrived in Padju Epat and said that I was there to study their *adat*, the people of the area thought this the most logical thing in the world, since they themselves find *adat* such a source of interest. Whenever I was sitting in on or getting the details of a case, I would be asked what the American *adat* code would call for in a similar situation. My answer would be discussed in a sympathetic but objective way, as those present would try to understand the social ramifications of the American *adat* system.

The Padju Epaters have a pragmatic attitude toward their legal system. They are happier discussing the particular details and extenuating circumstances of individual cases rather than articles of law in the abstract. They are also particularly open-minded. I was once discussing *adat* laws governing marriage between individuals of adjacent generations with the *adat* head of Murutuwu. Such marriages require a ritual fine, and the *adat* head listed several types of intergenerational marriage with the fine appropriate to each. As an after-thought, he mentioned father–daughter marriage. Looking for a symmetrical configuration, I asked him about mother–son marriage. He considered this, and stated that since there was no *adat* regulation concerning it, and since he knew of no cases involving it, he would have to withhold judgment on the matter until he had an actual case in hand that could be judged upon its particularistic merits. Thus anything, new or old, is open to *adat* adjudication when the circumstances require.

Adat Law and the National Legal System

Traditionally the Padju Epat *adat* legal system provided the machinery for adjudicating any type of restitutive or testimonial case. In criminal cases the accent was on restitution plus damages rather than on punishment. Any crime could be expiated through the payment of an assessed fine; even cases involving murder would be adjudicated in such a spirit. Although there were instances when kinsmen of a murdered man might refuse compensation and seek extralegal revenge, the pressure of community sentiment was almost always directed toward the accomplishment of an equitable and peaceful settlement of all disputes. Cases involving murder and similar crimes are now placed under police jurisdiction, but a resumé of a recent Padju Sapuluh *adat* case from Tamiang Layang may give an indication of pragmatic and equitable solutions that can be worked out in serious cases. A man, an only son, was accidentally killed by a spear trap while walking through the forest. The government authorities allowed the matter to be settled in an *adat* hearing. The elders had the owner of the trap pay a large fine and arranged for him to be adopted into the family of the dead man, so that the defendant would contribute support to the family of the deceased.

A few local lawsuits involving ownership of rubber trees have recently been taken to the civil rather than the *adat* court. However, because of Padju Epat's isolation and the slow working of civil court procedures, this is a rarely used facility. Generally speaking, voluntary recourse to the civil courts is taken only where litigation involves a Padju Epater and an outsider, where the disputed property lies outside Padju Epat territory, or where one of the litigants has a close relative in the government who can "look after" his case.

Weakening of the Adat Legal System

In the present day, there are some indications that the *adat* legal system is weakening in response to pressures from the modern world. The deterrent force of fines has lessened with inflation of the Indonesian economy. With the exception of Murutuwu, Padju Epat's *adat* heads were finding it harder and harder to carry out their duties because of the difficulties entailed in getting together enough elders to make a legal decision possible.

A case from Siong may illustrate some of the problems involved in the adjudication procedure at the current time. After the *idjambe* cremation ceremony was completed in Siong in July 1963, the Siong cemetery was empty. A month or so later, when a small swidden plot was being cleared adjacent to the cemetery, a fire got out of control and burned part of the cemetery area.

The burning of a cemetery, whether by mistake or design, constitutes a fairly serious offense in the *adat* legal system, and several Siongers tried to bring charges against the perpetrator on behalf of the community. The accusers stated that since the cemetery had been burned, a fine would have to be paid and a pig killed for purification. The individual responsible for the fire claimed that since there had been no bodies buried in the cemetery at the time of the incident, there had been no breach of *adat* law. The case was complicated by the fact that the defendant and plaintiffs respectively represented contending factions in Siong's social and political field. Several times a meeting was scheduled to hear the case, but on each occasion only one or two elders showed up and the *adat* head himself did not put in an appearance. Nobody was anxious to get caught in a factional squabble.

The matter came to a head when an old Siong lady died the following October. Her family did not want to place her in the Siong cemetery until it had been purified. At the same time, the exigencies of tropical climate dictated that the old lady be laid to rest with all possible dispatch. The matter was to be discussed on the second day of the two-day pre-burial ceremony. When the time came, however, the majority of the Siong elders were still conspicuous by their absence. With their exception, the obsequy was well attended. The guests included a number of elders from Telang and Murutuwu, some of whom were related to the deceased woman. The discussion was opened, and elders from the other villages invited to participate. One of the visiting *adat* heads gave a quiet, biting speech, couched in allegorical but unambiguous phrases, roasting the absent elders for their dereliction of duty in such a pressing case. This sentiment seemed widely shared among the visiting elders, but nonetheless, the latter felt that they could not try the case in the absence of their Siong confreres and the defendant in the case. It was finally decided that for the sake of expediency, the ritual fine and the sacrificial animal would be contributed by the family of the dead woman. This procedure would purify the graveyard so that the corpse could be buried and it was hoped, though not optimistically, that the bereaved family would be able to recover the costs of the ceremony from the man responsible for the original burning. This complex case had still not been resolved when I left Padju Epat six months later.

Moslems, Christians, and the Adat Legal Code

By distinguishing between the belief system and the legal system of Kaharinganism, Padju Epat's Moslems have been able to establish a satisfactory *modus vivendi* with their animist neighbors. Within the family, the tenets of Islam are followed. In the wider sphere of village life, if a Moslem finds himself in a position where an *adat* fine is called for, he pays the fine, but has a *Kaharingan* friend kill the required animal and perform any necessary purification with its blood. Thus the Moslems tacitly recognize the importance of the *adat* legal code as a device for maintaining order within the community. Where an *adat* regulation is not specifically ruled out by Islamic law, it should be observed, with the modifications mentioned above.

Unfortunately, this is a viewpoint that is not necessarily shared by some recent converts to Christianity. Many of these neophyte Christians feel that having ostensibly shed their "pagan" beliefs, they are no longer bound by any part of the *adat* legal code. Although this attitude is deplored by the older Christians in the community, who advocate a compromise similar to that adopted by the Moslems, it has led to some conflicts with the animist community. For instance, under one *adat* regulation, if a rice field is cleared that straddles both sides of a public thoroughfare, either a path or a stream, a small fine should be paid and a ceremony given in which the thoroughfare is purified through *pilah*. This will enable the rice spirit to get across from one part of the field to another. If the ceremony is not given, it is not the owner of the field who will suffer, but the people who use the path or stream. In Telang there was a Christian who had cleared a field covered by the regulation. He refused to give the ceremony on the grounds that he was a Christian, which was reasonable, but he also refused to have a *Kaharingan* give the ceremony, on the grounds that it was a Christian field. The *Kaharingan* community considered the Christian's behavior not only highly unreasonable, but also quite dangerous as well, since the field in question straddled a heavily used new road leading into Center Telang. Much pressure was brought to bear on the recalcitrant individual by both *Kaharingan* and elders in the Christian congregation. However, Padju Epaters are an individualistic lot and tend to get obstinate under public pressure. The Christian at the center of the controversy got stubborn, and all attempts to have the affair adjudicated were unsuccessful, at least until the time I left the area.

7

Village, Hamlet, and Emigre Settlements

ALTHOUGH RECOGNIZED BOTH BY ITS OWN PEOPLE and by outsiders as one major segment within the larger Ma'anyan tribe, Padju Epat is by no means an integrated political unit. Rather, it is an aggregate of individual villages which are loosely bound together by geographical contiguity, an awareness of common origins, and a core of shared traditions (*adat*). In the governmental hierarchy, the territory of Padju Epat has long been treated as an administrative unit: it first became a district under Dutch colonial rule, and in modern Indonesia the subdistrict of Padju Epat stands at the lowest level of the national government bureaucracy.

Several of Padju Epat's villages may choose to act in concert on some specific project, or more likely they may be urged to cooperate by the local government representative. Nonetheless, each Padju Epat village is a politically independent corporation. Each has its own traditional farming territory, its own village officers and adjudicating elders, and its own body of specialized tradition (*adat*). In addition, certain ceremonial cycles are fulfilled within the village context. Obligatory mortuary rites, especially the burdensome cremation ceremonies, are performed jointly by the members of a village.

Village Territory

Each Padju Epat village has its own traditional territory within the district's approximately 112 square miles. Boundaries are marked by some natural feature, usually a stream. The land area is not equally divided among the five villages: Telang's territory covers about 38, Siong's 34, Murutuwu's 17, Balawa's 17, and Kararat's 6, square miles. In Telang and Siong, however, much land lies within the Barito flood zone; there are more marshes and sandy areas than in Murutuwu, Balawa, or Kararat, and their land generally seems less fertile. However, the territories of Telang and Siong do offer greater economic diversification, since fishing is better and access to cash timberlands is easier.

Village Government

The internal affairs of each Padju Epat community should be administered by a group of village officers, some elected and some appointed. Ideally,

53

each village has a complement of officers that includes a village head, an assistant village head, a village crier, a secretary, a swidden manager, a forest manager, an *adat* head, an assistant *adat* head, and an *adat* investigator. Almost all of these posts, as currently constituted, seem to have been creations of either the Dutch or Indonesian governments.

The most important posts are those of village head and *adat* head. The first serves as village administrator and leader, and the latter, as described above, is the senior *adat* law adjudicator. Both officers are supposed to be elected, with all male villagers over eighteen eligible to vote. The other officers are appointed by the village head and the *adat* head.

In pre-Dutch times, each Padju Epat village had a single leader, who served as a consensus spokesman for the village, somewhat like today's *adat* head. When the Dutch assumed practical control of the Ma'anyan area in the nineteenth century, new administrative functions were assigned to the village head, who became increasingly preoccupied with these duties to the detriment of his adjudicative role. Around 1914, to handle local *adat* disputes, the Dutch created the office of *adat* head. Thus, under Dutch influence, the traditional duties of the village head were divided between two functionaries, the village head and the *adat* head.

The village head (*pambakal*) is a village-level government official, entitled for his services to receive a token honorarium from the provincial government. He is responsible for the welfare of his village and for maintaining order; he is supposed to collect an annual poll tax from all men over eighteen years of age. He should keep a registry of births and deaths, a list of village residents, and maintain any other necessary records. The village head has authority to issue permits so that outsiders may farm in the territory of his village; it is also his duty to organize cooperative labor groups for public works projects. To qualify for the post of village head, an individual should be literate, own his own house, and have personal influence in the village. Since at the present time the responsibilities of office are wearisome and the rewards slight, it also helps to be financially well-to-do. In most Padju Epat villages today the position is considered an empty honor coupled with irksome duties, and it is more vigorously avoided than sought. Given this reluctant public attitude, it is often difficult for a village to find a willing candidate who meets the requirements of office.

The other village offices have little meaning. Only Murutuwu had a village secretary, a junior high school graduate who kept the minutes of all village assemblies and also did a lot of the village head's paperwork. There was a group of educated young men in Murutuwu who felt that it was progressive to run village meetings according to their equivalent of Roberts' Rules of Order, to make speeches in a rather opaque style that passed for official Indonesian, and to keep notes on everything. For the Murutuwu village secretary, his incumbency gave him a chance to practice for greater future responsibilities. The other villages did not bother with a secretary, although during the cremation ceremony in 1963, Siong had a temporary secretary, a well educated emigre, to handle the paper work generated by the ceremony.

The duties of village crier (*pangerak*) involve much unpleasant work and little glory. When the village head has any announcements to be made, the crier bustles around the village spreading the news. If a public works project is getting under way, he is supposed to collect the laborers needed. It is not a sought-after job, but several villages carried criers on their official rosters.

The swidden manager (*kapala padang*) is supposed to keep agricultural statistics for the village and record the location, size, and yield of each swidden plot in use. Although three villages had swidden managers, they apparently served in name only. A swidden manager may be called upon to testify in an *adat* legal case involving a dispute over swidden rights. One of the swidden managers held the post of forest manager concurrently.

The forest manager (*kapala hutan*) is supposed to supervise the exploitation of forest products, including the cutting of rattan, the planting of rubber, and the felling of trees for commercial use. Since almost all commercial forest exploitation requires a permit from the subdistrict officer, his office has tended to take over the important duties of the forest manager. To my knowledge, only two villages had individuals serving in this capacity.

The position of *adat* head was the only village officer post that still carried much prestige. In Telang and Siong, the village governmental apparatus was moribund. The heads of these two villages, operating under the administrative shadow cast by Padju Epat's subdistrict officer, felt inhibited by the latter's close proximity and allowed most of the responsibility for village government to pass to him. The more distant villages did not feel so constrained by the presence of the subdistrict officer. Kararat, however, had too small a population to support a full complement of village officers, and had only a headman. As the latter explained the situation, "If we're going to elect officers in this small village, who's going to be left to be the people?" While only Murutuwu carried a full slate of village officers, both this village and Balawa managed to maintain a relatively effective and autonomous system of village government, a state of affairs engendering conscious pride among the inhabitants of these two villages. On the whole, however, the official government apparatus in Padju Epat was in a state of decay during my stay in the area.

Types of Settlements

There is some evidence that Padju Epaters did not traditionally dwell in permanent villages. Colonial records seem to indicate that the first centralized settlements in the region were established only a little more than a century ago, in 1856, at the behest of the Dutch administration. Prior to that time, Padju Epaters lived in isolated field houses or small temporary hamlets near their swidden plots.

All of Padju Epat's current villages probably began as swidden hamlets settled either from the ancient village of Halaman or from Telang. In past times, according to traditional history, some hamlets were quite large, having their own cemeteries, ceremonial halls, cremation structures, and *tambak*. However, according to customary law, such settlements were technically not villages but permanent hamlets known as *tumpungan.*

In order to comprehend fully the dynamics of social organization in Padju Epat today, it is necessary to understand the distinctions that exist among three types of settlement: there is the true village (*tumpuk*), such as Telang or Murutuwu; there is the permanent hamlet (*tumpungan*); and there is the the temporary swidden hamlet (*bantai*).

The true village (*tumpuk*) has its own territory; it has its own headman, customary law head, and adjudicating elders; it has a ceremonial hall, a cremation structure, and *tambak;* it has land and water village guardian statues; and a number of its houses have individual protective ancestral spirits called *nanyu'.*

A permanent hamlet (*tumpungan*) has many of the characteristics of a real village. It may have a resident population that is equal to or greater than a true village. It may have a headman, customary law head, adjudicating elders, ceremonial hall, cremation structure, and *tambak.* But it has no village spirits, no guardian statues, and no ancestral spirits, and these are the spirits that offer protection to a village's population.

In order to raise its status from permanent hamlet to true village, a settlement must give a costly ceremony called *gawe,* which honors Dewata, a crocodile spirit. According to legend, a maiden named Siris Gading Lusun married Dewata when his spirit was in the shape of a man. She was then carried off to her husband's watery kingdom. The girl's parents were understandably upset, being afraid that they would never see her again. However, Siris Gading Lusun sent word to her father and mother, saying that if they wanted to see her again, they should give the ceremony called *gawe.* The girl then instructed them in the necessary ritual and making of the required paraphernalia. During the *gawe* ceremony a water guardian statue (*tungkup*) is made and placed in the river, and this becomes Dewata's residence when he returns for the annual spirit propitiation ceremony, *mira ka'ayat.* When *gawe* is given, a spiritual protective shield is put around the settlement's territory so that enemies and sickness may not enter. Only after a settlement has given *gawe* may it erect land guardian statues and houses for ancestral spirits; only then does it become a true village.

A temporary swidden hamlet (*bantai*) has none of the accoutrements of a village or permanent hamlet, although it may have an officially designated headman. It is merely a temporary agglomeration of nuclear families who decide to be neighbors for a year or two. One of the advantages of the swidden hamlet relationship is that the hamlet's constituent families form the nucleus for a labor exchange force. During the period when the rice crop is ripening, one or two individuals can guard a number of contiguous fields by using a series of mechanical bird and animal scarers that can be activated from a central elevated location by means of strings. This arrangement makes it possible for even an understaffed family to guard its hamlet swidden while also looking after its other fields, since many families have several, often widely separated plots.

Although it may have been possible for a temporary hamlet in the Padju Epat area to become a permanent hamlet or even a village a century or more ago, this is no longer the case. The swidden hamlet in Padju Epat's home territory is now ephemeral; a given hamlet will remain intact, at best, for no more than three or four years. Then it will break up, with some of its constituent families staying together to form the nucleus for a new hamlet elsewhere in the village territory. Other families may move their base of operations back to the village for a year or two, or perhaps decide they have had enough of people for awhile, and seek some isolated spot. For the Padju Epater craves variety; variety in his daily activities, variety in his domicile, and variety in his neighbors. And after a year or two of hamlet life, he wants a change. Thus, the associations between individuals and between families are periodically altered, readjusted, and rearranged.

Emigre Villages

The distinction among village, permanent hamlet, and temporary hamlet is no longer too meaningful in the local Padju Epat context. However, it is important with relation to Padju Epat's ties with many areas of the eastern Barito region lying to the north. Today, most of Padju Epat's hamlet settlements are located outside Padju Epat territory, scattered here and there in the drainages of the Paku, Karau, Buntok, and Ayuh rivers.

I have indicated that the soil of Padju Epat is not overly fertile, although it does support the existing population. There is some indication that the effective resident population of Padju Epat has changed very little over the last hundred years. In 1857, the population of the region was estimated to be 834, which is almost precisely the same as the 1963 population (excluding Tampulangit), which was 846. My analysis of the childbearing histories of Padju Epat's women gives evidence that the population has been gradually increasing, at least over the last sixty-five years.

Even in the 1850's, it was reported that overpopulation forced some Padju Epaters to seek agricultural land to the north, in the drainages of the Paku and Karau rivers, which lay in the traditional hilly territory of Lawangan Dayaks. The Lawangan region had an extremely low population density and fertile land covered mostly by primary forest. In the nineteenth century, an immense tract of swidden land could be rented for a pittance.

The land in the Paku and Karau drainages was not only good for agriculture, but its forests were well stocked with many varieties of commercial timber, some of which were already being exploited by Padju Epat canoe makers in the mid-nineteenth century. In fact, according to local informants, it was the quest for "canoe trees" that first led Padju Epaters into the Paku–Karau area after the Dutch had pacified the area to a certain extent. There had once been a special practice of distant journeying in search of forest products, especially timber for canoes. Such a trip was mostly a task for young men, who would travel north during the dry season to cut timber and make canoes to be floated out during the rainy season and taken to Bandjarmasin for sale. Men following this line of endeavor were often away from the village for six months or a year at a time. Frequently during these trips, men would note a patch of good agricultural land where, at a later time, an agricultural hamlet might be established.

The Lawangans of the Paku–Karau region had a well deserved reputation as fierce, roving warriors; the earliest Padju Epat settlements along the Paku River were large, and thus reasonably safe from attack. In the early decades of the twentieth century, with the opening of the Dutch road linking Telang with Dayu, Tampa, and Ampah in the north, and with Tamiang Layang and Bandjarmasin in the southeast, the Paku–Karau region became a relatively safe area, as long as one did not stray too far into the hills. In the last sixty years, Padju Epat emigre settlements have blossomed in a number of places in the Paku–Karau region and even further to the north in the Ayuh River drainage. (The locations of some of the larger Padju Epat emigre communities are marked by dots on Map B.)

Emigre Ties to Padju Epat

Neither the temporary nor the permanent hamlet was wholly independent, and their members maintained ties with the home village in Padju Epat. Some emigre settlements certainly have endured for many years. A number of individuals now living in Padju Epat were born in these communities, and some reported that their families had been living in a particular permanent hamlet for three or four generations. According to older informants, after completing their harvests, the emigres used to return to their Padju Epat villages. Such visits must have been brief, since before long the need to clear swiddens for the next agricultural year would have taken them back to their distant hamlets. Many people who spent most of their adult lives farming in the north would then come home to Padju Epat to "retire." Sentimental attachment for the home village may partially account for the persistence of these ties; the desire to see relatives also brought some people back, although more close relatives probably lived in the vicinity of their up-country settlements. At any rate, the strength of these affective ties begins to fade after a generation or so.

A legal fiction in the Dutch administrative system also served to bind emigres to their home villages. Partly to simplify the collection of taxes, the Dutch did not like to recognize the existence of the emigre communities and continued to census and tax all individuals in their Padju Epat villages of origin, whether they resided there or not. Thus, one elderly informant, a former local official, stated that in the early 1920's there were over 1,000 individuals on Telang's tax lists, which included all males over the age of eighteen, although there were no more than 200 taxables actually living in the village. The rest lived up-country in emigre settlements. Another informant, who had served as Siong's village head between 1941 and 1946, recalled that it was not until

1943 during the Japanese occupation that emigre taxables were shifted to the lists of their respective up-country settlements. There were 199 taxables and 1,337 people counted in Siong in 1941, whereas in 1946, only 50 taxables were left.

The most important factor binding the emigre to his home village in Padju Epat, however, was the necessity to fulfill certain ceremonial obligations. None of the emigre communities rates as a true village, for none has given the *gawe* ceremony. Thus, none of these settlements has village protectors in the form of guardian statues, and none of the individual houses in these settlements has homes for ancestral spirits. All protective spirits must be fed annually in the post-harvest thanksgiving ceremony *mira ka'ayat*. It was the celebration of this ritual that used to bring emigres back to Padju Epat every year following their harvests. An ancestral spirit (*nanyu'*) in the family's "home" household, especially, was not one to be neglected, for in the absence of guardian statues, who only have power in the home territory of their own villages, the ancestral spirit is the most important spiritual protector of his descendants living up-country. But the *nanyu'* feels protective only toward those descendants who feed him.

Obligatory mortuary rites formed an even stronger ceremonial bond linking the emigre with his home village. Prior to 1962, when an *idjambe* cremation ceremony was held in the emigre community of Bondar, none of the up-country settlements had ceremonial halls, cremation structures, or *tambak*. In the early days they did not even have cemeteries, but brought their dead back to Padju Epat for primary burial; later they returned to celebrate *idjambe*. Today, a few corpses are still brought back for primary burial, but most are interred in their hamlet cemeteries. Even so, the bones of most animist emigres who still follow Padju Epat custom are returned to their home village for cremation.

The ceremonial need to return to the home village for *idjambe* has helped perpetuate ties between the Padju Epat villages and their emigre families over the years. However, as the affective bonds linking the emigre to his home village have grown weaker with time, the requirement of maintaining ceremonial ties has become more burdensome, not only in terms of the necessary economic outlay, but because of the distances that have to be covered and the time taken away from subsistence activities in the up-country settlement. For a young man of Gagutur on the Ayuh River, it is an onerous task to exhume the bones of a parent, carry them fifty miles to Siong, which he may never have visited before, and in cooperation with a group of seeming strangers, put on a nine-day ceremony with which he has little familiarity.

Within the last few years two innovations have developed that will weaken even the ceremonial bonds linking the emigre communities to the Padju Epat villages. *Mia*, one of the death ceremonies first established for the headless corpses of Sarunai and later adopted by the non-Padju Epat Ma-'anyan after the destruction of their cremation structures by Labai Lumiah, is reported to be gaining favor among Padju Epat emigres. *Mia* is not a cremation ceremony, and it does not require a ceremonial hall, cremation structure, or *tambak*. The idea of this ceremony is anathema to the older and more traditionally minded, but others find it preferable to the effort and expense involved in following the *idjambe* cremation ceremony in Padju Epat.

The second innovation involved the establishment of a ceremonial hall, cremation structure, and a *tambak* at the emigre settlement of Bondar, the first such structures known to exist outside Padju Epat since the storied onslaught of Labai Lumiah. An *idjambe* cremation ceremony was first held in Bondar in June 1962 and a second was planned for late 1964, well after my departure. Even so, some of the more conservative Bondar residents did not approve of the innovation nor the general lack of expertise in the performance of the ritual there. In 1963 a number of Bondar people showed up for the cremation ceremonies held in Murutuwu and Siong carrying the remains of relatives who had died long before the Bondar ceremony, and thus eligible to have been included there.

For both emigres and resident Padju Epaters who find the ceremonial obligations of the traditional animist life becoming too burdensome, there is the third alternative of conversion to Christianity. Whether more emigre communities follow the example of Bondar and establish cremation facilities in their own settlements, whether they turn to the *mia* ceremony for the treatment of their dead, or convert to Christianity, their ties with the home villages in Padju Epat are likely to become increasingly attenuated with time.

8

Kinsmen and Kin Terms

LTHOUGH MANY OF ITS SONS AND DAUGHTERS have emigrated over the last few generations, few outsiders venture into Padju Epat on other than a temporary basis. The vast majority (94 percent) of people currently living within its borders were born in Padju Epat and, indeed, about 87 percent of the population continues to reside in the village of their birth. Given this statistical tendency toward village endogamy and the relatively small size of individual communities, the average Padju Epater operates in a social field in which most of his co-villagers are kinsmen related to him through either blood (consanguineal) or marriage (affinal) ties.

Kinship and Kin Groups in Padju Epat Society

Anthropologists have traditionally shown a keen interest in the analysis of kinship, since in many societies the principles regulating the relations among kinsmen are the most important ones governing the interaction of individuals within the society.

In Padju Epat, all the descendants of an individual's eight pairs of great-great grandparents are recognized as consanguineal kinsmen, and are designated by kin terms. The spouses of an individual's consanguineal relatives are also recognized as affinal kinsmen, as are certain of his or her spouse's consanguineal kinsmen. Not all of these affinal kinsmen are denoted by distinctive kin terms.

Within the general universe of kinsmen recognized by a Padju Epater, an individual will share special rights and obligations toward some on the basis of common membership in kin groups based on common descent and/or residence. The most important types of kin groups operating in Padju Epat society are the *dangau* family, the *lewu'* family, the *tambak* group, the *bumuh*, and the kindred.

The *dangau* family is the primary social, economic, and ritual unit in Padju Epat society. Its locus is a swidden field house (*dangau*), and its membership generally comprises a husband and wife, their unmarried children, and sometimes, on a temporary basis, a married child and his or her spouse and children.

The *lewu'* family is a residential unit with the village house (*lewu'*) as its locus. It owns heirloom property and mediates rights to swidden lands and *tambak* group affiliations. It comprises one or, more usually, several *dangau* families which are economically independent but which share common rights in the village house and the property under its control. The constituent *dangau* families are those of the *lewu'*s builders and/or the *dangau* families of the builders' descendants who have not taken up post-marital residence in some other household. Every *dangau* family is associated with a *lewu'* family.

A *tambak* group is a named kin group which has as its locus a *tambak* (or ironwood box) into which the ash residue of its members' remains is placed at the conclusion of the *idjambe* cremation ceremony. Each *tambak* has a founder or founders. The membership of the *tambak* group includes all of the founder's descendants, and their spouses, who have not become affiliated with some other *tambak* group. Unlike the *bumuh, tambak* groups are discrete and mutually exclusive, so that an individual can only belong to one at a time. A person initially gains membership in a *tambak* group at birth, but his *tambak* group affiliation may be changed through adoption or marriage. When a marriage between members of different *tambak* groups is being arranged, determination of the couple's post-marital *tambak* group affiliation is one of the important questions to be settled. *Tambak* groups own their associated *tambak* and heirloom property. Traditionally the *tambak* groups of a village were ranked relative to one another in a now mostly defunct system of class stratification.

The *bumuh* is a kin group that contains all the descendants of a particular ancestor. Thus, the *bumuh* is a bilineal descent group in which membership is transmitted through both men and women. The *bumuh* is not an exclusive group, and an individual can belong to as many different *bumuh* as he has lineal ancestors. A *bumuh* controls an estate inherited from its focal (i.e., founding) ancestor which may comprise land-use rights, fruit trees, houses, and heirloom property, although not all *bumuh* estates contain all of these assets. Since a *bumuh* may have many members with claims on its estate, *bumuh* rules provide a priority system for allocating the use of its property among its members. The members of the *lewu'* family associated with the *bumuh*'s progenitor have primary rights in the use of *bumuh* property. The bases upon which other *bumuh* members are assigned secondary, tertiary, and residual rights in the estate will be described at length in a later section.

The kindred is an Ego-centric set of kinsmen comprising the members of the eight maximal *bumuh*, descended from his eight pairs of great-great grandparents, to which an individual belongs. Dyadic kin ties link an individual with the various individual members of his kindred. These ties may be either active or inactive. Those members of his kindred with whom he maintains active dyadic ties have an obligation to assist him in various activities and he, in return, has an obligation to help each of them in the performance of similar activities. Those members of his kindred, perhaps the greater number, with whom he maintains inactive dyadic ties, provide the individual with a vast pool of latent kinsmen with whom he may establish active ties should the need arise.

In analyzing any kinship system, one of the first objects of study is the kinship terminology used to designate the rather few categories to which individual kinsmen are assigned from the viewpoint of a hypothetical focal individual usually termed "ego," for there is no society in which every individual kinsman that Ego recognizes is accorded a separate, distinctive kin term. Having found the categories designated by distinctive kin terms, it is then necessary to find the principles used by Ego, and presumably by other members of the community, to assign individual kinsmen to their proper categories. Then the investigator seeks to determine the types of behavior that characterize the relations between an Ego and his kinsmen designated by the same kin term. With minor variations, the people of Padju Epat categorize their kinsmen and apply their kin terms in much the same way that we do in the United States.

Terms of Reference

It is customary for anthropologists to distinguish between the way in which kin terms are applied when talking *about* a particular kinsman (terms of reference) and when talking *to* a kinsman (terms of address). The system by which kin terms are applied referentially is generally given priority in the study of kinship terminology. The description contained in this section pertains to terms of reference.

In Padju Epat, Ego's eight pairs of great-great grandparents and all their descendants are recognized as consanguineal (blood) kinsmen. These kinsmen, extending four generations above and four generations below Ego and including cousins to the third degree, are grouped into several categories, each denoted by a distinctive kin term. In Ego's own generation, the kin categories recognized are *tata'* ("elder sibling"), *ani'* ("younger sibling"), and *tuwari* ("cousin"). Where more precision is required, cousins of the first, second, and third degree may be referred to by the descriptive terms *sahinra'an* (*sahinra'* "once"), *sanruehan* (*sanrueh* "twice"), and *santeluan* (*santelu* "thrice") respectively. Even where genealogical connections are known to exist, cousins beyond the third degree are not considered kinsmen. In the generation above Ego are recognized *ineh* ("mother"), *ambah* ("father"), *tutu'* ("aunt", i.e., parent's sister and parent's first or second female cousin), and *mama'* ("uncle", i.e., parent's brother and parent's first or second male cousin). In the second ascendent generation *nini'* ("grandmother" and grandparent's sister or female first cousin) and *kakah* ("grandfather" and grandparent's brother or male first cousin) are recognized. In the third generation above Ego, *datu'* ("great grandparent" and great grandparent's sibling) is recognized, while in the fourth ascending generation all great-great grandparents are termed *munyang*. In the generation below Ego, his own children of both sexes are termed *ia*, while the children of his siblings are termed *aken*. Only one kin category each in the second, third, and fourth descendent generations is recognized: *umpu* ("grand-child"), *buyut* ("great grandchild"), and *entah* ("great-great grandchild").

There are only seven terms used to identify affinal categories of kins-men. In the first ascending generation *kasian* ("spouse's parent") and in the first descending generation *nantu* ("child's spouse") are recognized. In Ego's own generation the affinal categories denoted by terms are *darangan* ("spouse"), *iwan* ("spouse's sister" and "brother's wife"), *daup* ("spouse's brother" and "sister's husband"), *sanrui* ("spouse's sibling's spouse"), and *bulau* ("child's spouse's parent"). In the generations above Ego's, consanguineal terms are extended to include the spouses of collateral kinsmen, with due regard for the criteria of age and sex. Thus, as in the United States, the husband of a parent's sister (*tutu'*) is termed an uncle (*mama'*), and the wife of a parent's brother (*mama'*), an aunt (*tutu'*). Similarly, the wife of a *kakah* is termed a *nini'*, and the husband of a *nini'* is termed a *kakah*.

Terms of Address

Kin terms, rather than names, are frequently used when talking to kinsmen. Terms that denote kinsmen genealogically close to Ego in the refer-ential system are often extended to include more distant kinsmen of the same generation. Thus the terms for mother (*ineh*) and father (*ambah*) may be used when addressing a parent's sister or brother. In fact, so pervasive is the use of kin terms for address, that they are frequently extended to include nonkinsmen as well. The higher the generation of an individual above Ego, the wider the extension of close kin terms. Almost any villager of the grand-parental generation will be addressed as *kakah* or *nini'*. When speaking to individuals in descendent generations, the practice varies with the status of the individual addressed. Young children are more frequently addressed by name than by a kin term. Individuals who are already married and have families are almost always addressed by another term that anthropologists call a teknonym.

The Use of Teknonymy

A teknonym is a term by which a person is referred to or addressed as the parent of a particular child, or, later, as the grandparent of a certain grandchild. Padju Epat's system of teknonymy is fairly simple, though its use does present certain obstacles to the ethnographer trying to sort out genealo-gies and individual relationships. Shortly after an individual is born, he or she receives a personal name, such as Agun, Likup, Serep, or perhaps something up-to-date like Atom or Plastik. These are the names used until a person has married and had a child. After this child has been named, and let us call him Ater, his parents are thereafter known as Father of Ater (Pa'Ater) and Mother of Ater (either Ineh Ater or Tu'Ater). On the birth of a grandchild, whom we shall name Tehur, the teknonym is changed once again. The grandparents become known as Kakah Tehur ("grandfather of Tehur") and Nini' Tehur ("grandmother of Tehur"). The sex of the child from whom a teknonym is derived is immaterial, and names are taken from either a boy or a girl. Since an individual does not really attain adult status until he has offspring, a childless couple will usually adopt a child and therefrom attain the teknonyms that mark their change in status. Thus an individual may be known by three different names at three different stages in his life. For the outsider, there is a little confusion, since the parental teknonym may continue to be used by force of habit even after the grandparental teknonym has been acquired. It does not appear that teknonyms are taken from great grandchildren.

Teknonyms are used both as terms of reference and as forms of address. After an individual has acquired a teknonym, there is a certain reluctance on the part of others to use his personal name, at least as a form of address. As terms of reference, personal names are still used on occasion. Informants would freely tell me the personal names of almost anyone they knew, although younger members of the community often did not know the birth names of the elderly. There was a definite avoidance in the use of personal names, both in reference and address, for mothers- and fathers-in-law; otherwise there is no actual *adat* prohibition on the use of birth names. But, as we might hesitate to address an established member of the community by a foolish childhood nickname, the Padju Epaters feel that birth names are incongruent with the individual's present status in the world. The only adults who were consistently known by their personal names were people who had disabilities making them unfit for marriage. In one village there were several unmarried simple-minded men in their thirties and forties who, although pleasant and hard-working members of the community, were still called by their personal names, assigning them more or less the status of children.

The Application of Kin Terms

There is much individual variation in the application of kinship terms and teknonyms. One person may have a penchant for extending primary kin terms to practically anybody, while another does so sparingly. One person will address a father's cousin by teknonym, where another would use the term "uncle." This is a matter of personal style. Then, too, a single individual will, at different times, use variant styles of address or reference for the same person. In general, affinal terms are not extended in the manner common to consanguineal terms. An exception to this is the extension of the term for sister's husband or spouse's brother (*daup*) as a jesting term of address for a suspected or self-proclaimed womanizer.

The Generational Component

The most important function of Padju Epat kin terms is to assign the people that they denote to the proper generation relative to Ego. There is no doubt that among all the Ma'anyan kin terms, the generational component is the most pervasive structural feature. The formal distinction between generations is maintained in the general extension of kin terms, and kin terms suitable to one generation are never extended to individuals belonging to another generation. Due to demographic vicissitudes, forty years in age may separate the youngest son of a youngest son from his cousin, the oldest son of an oldest son. Yet if the younger wishes to use a kin term for the elder, his choice is limited to "older brother," "cousin," or "first cousin," depending upon how precisely he wants to define the relationship. In cases where there is such an extreme disparity in ages, however, the younger man would rarely use a kin term to denote or address the other. Instead, he would use the latter's teknonym (either Pa'_____ or Kakah_____) so that respect for the elder's age could be connoted without compromising the principle of generational identity.

Generational integrity is also maintained in the institution of marriage. A marriage in which the husband and wife belong to terminologically adjacent generations is theoretically proscribed by *adat* law. However, as with so many *adat* proscriptions, such a marriage can be regularized by the payment of an appropriate fine.

Ideal Behavior toward Kinsmen

As there is a certain amount of individual and situational variation in the application of kin terms, there is similar variety in the way in which kinsmen behave toward each other. Nevertheless, there are certain institutionalized modes of behavior that ideally regulate relations between different classes of kinsmen. Here the generational component again has the widest applicability in the governance of such behavior. The ideal attitudes prescribe overt deference toward persons of higher generation and a somewhat paternalistic posture toward persons of lower generation. The degree of deference or paternalism that is appropriate to show toward a kinsman is, theoretically, directly proportional to the number of generations that separate him from Ego. Within Ego's own generation, this deference–paternalism dimension is rescaled to the values of relative age, with deference toward older real and classificatory siblings and paternalism toward younger ones.

As children, older siblings, whether male or female, are expected to, and in practice do, spend a considerable amount of time looking after younger brothers and sisters. It was common among some Telang and Siong families who maintained distant swiddens to leave young school-age children in the village for days at a time, in the care of an older sibling. Ideally the older ones exercise their powers with restraint, while for their part, the younger ones obey, as best children can, without feeling unduly oppressed. In general, the bonds between siblings are very close ones, cemented by real affection, and they remain intact throughout a lifetime, though they may become attenuated by geographical separation. Behavior toward cousins is similar to that between siblings, although the warmth with which the relationship is embued may become attenuated with second and third cousins. Cousins who have a close personal relationship usually address one another by the sibling terms appropriate to their relative ages.

The relationship between parents and children, though following the basic paternalism–deference pattern, is also strongly suffused with affection. Children of both sexes are valued and receive equal loving attention from their parents. The disciplining of smaller children (which is minimal and permissive to the extreme) and the responsibility for maintaining discipline is borne not only by the parents, but in the multi-family village houses, by resident aunts, uncles, and older siblings as well. Until the age of four or five years, children of both sexes receive much the same treatment. However, as children grow older and begin to perform useful activities commensurate with their youthful abilities, boys spend more time with their fathers and girls with their mothers, each learning the technological specialties assigned to his sex. As children become adults and the economic equals of their parents, they become independent, and the dominant–subordinate aspects of the relationship disappear for all practical purposes. However, the formal aspects of the paternalism–deference relationship are maintained. Even when a young family man has already decided on a particular course of action, he will go through the motions of conferring with his parents, or his parents-in-law, if he has taken up uxorilocal residence. Parents expect to be consulted by their children on important matters. Some oldsters do give a continuous stream of gratuitous advice to their children, but the majority follow the ideal path of offering counsel only when it is requested, even though they may feel slighted on certain occasions.

The relationship between an individual and his parents' siblings is ideally a close and warm one. However, in actual practice, the content of the relationship shows considerable variation, depending on the personal characteristics and background of the specific individuals involved. In one case I recorded, a young married girl turned to her uncle for help against her parents. The girl's husband came from an emigre settlement. After their marriage, the young couple took up uxorilocal residence with the girl's family, but her parents did not like her husband and tried to force a divorce. The girl and her husband, who were happy together, ran off to another village, where they took up residence with her father's brother. This uncle felt that the couple should not be parted if they wanted to stay married, and had the case reviewed by his village's adjudicating elders. The elders concurred in upholding the marriage and arranged a rapprochement between the couple and the girl's parents. This was effected, and the couple returned to the wife's home village. At the opposite end of the spectrum, there was an instance in which a woman engaged in a bitter dispute with her sister's son over the ownership of some rubber trees, and eventually was responsible for sending her nephew to jail. This was admittedly an unusual case, and was considered quite atypical by other villagers. Nonetheless, it illustrates the degree of variation from ideal behavior that can be found where particular individuals, as opposed to general categories of kinsmen, are involved.

The relationship between grandparents and grandchildren is perhaps the warmest one in the catalogue. Older people love to be with their grandchildren. They are very indulgent toward them, and since the grandparents have little responsibility for the disciplining of their grandchildren, very little conflict enters into the relationship. For the grandparents, the establishment and maintenance of close ties with at least some of their grandchildren has a practical as well as an affective dimension.

In Padju Epat, an individual's primary responsibilities after marriage are to his family of procreation and only secondarily to his natal family. Consequently, a married couple can ordinarily expect regular assistance in their work only from close kinsmen who are unmarried. In the early and middle phases of their married life, a couple receives a great deal of assistance from its own children. After these children have grown up and married, unmarried grandchildren, and eventually great-grandchildren, prove the best potential source of assistance for an old couple. For the purpose of providing this assistance, married children who have left their natal families are morally obligated to make their own children available for "grandparent service."

Padju Epaters recognize that children, being children, can be capricious and inconstant. A child dispatched to assist grandparents in some activity may or may not render willing service. Padju Epaters realize that much depends on the quality of the personal relationship that exists between the elder people and the grandchild. Where a warm affective relationship is found, conscientious service can be anticipated. Where a neutral or strained relationship exists, indifferent service is to be expected. Older people are anxious to establish, wherever possible, particularly close personal ties with one or two grandchildren, and it is felt that it is never too early to initiate this sort of relationship. Thus, a Padju Epater's natural fondness for grandchildren is augmented by the knowledge that a comfortable old age depends, to a great extent, on the good will of his grandchildren. The solicitous treatment of particular grandchildren begins almost at birth with special attentions that the child's own parents may be unable to provide. One four-year-old child of a widowed mother lived with his great-grandparents in Telang. The boy was not then capable of rendering much assistance, but with the passage of time, his usefulness would steadily increase. Thus, the services of a fairly attentive helper seemed guaranteed to the old couple for the ensuing fifteen or so years.

It may be seen then, that the establishment of a close affective tie with particular grandchildren is an investment in a type of social security. Where this kind of relationship is initiated with a young child, there is an expectation that the latter will be disposed to render attentive service to an aging grandparental couple. However, it is expected that such personal services will be largely terminated when the child has married and established his own family of procreation. Thus it is necessary that the old folks establish similar personal relationships with at least one or two children in each succeeding generation. For this reason, where they survive, the relationships obtaining between great-grandparents and their descendants is about the same as that for grandparents. The members of the senior generation are not the sole beneficiaries from this special grandparent–grandchild relationship, since grandparents can be counted on to care for grandchildren who come from families broken by death or divorce.

The relationship between spouses is rather one of equals in a business partnership. Each has a contribution to make to the family economy, and both are expected to be industrious. Though the husband is usually the spokesman for both, he is expected to consult with his wife on all important matters. If not consulted, a wife usually will not be shy about offering her opinion. As in a business partnership, affection is not a necessary ingredient in the relationship. For those who find their spouses unacceptable, divorce is fairly easy and carries little or no social opprobrium. However, an individual who has a hardworking spouse will usually overlook many defects before seeking relief in divorce. In three villages there were several cases of couples who had been married for two or three decades, but who had barely spoken to each other in years. This was, however, an unusual situation, and even in arranged marriages, affection comes with children and mutual adjustment. In over 60 percent of the marriages current in the villages of Telang, Siong, and Murutuwu, neither spouse had been married more than once.

The relationships that exist between an individual and his spouse's kinsmen generally parallel those with his consanguineal kinsmen, especially if he or she follows his spouse in marriage. In the early stages of marriage, an attitude of reticence typifies the behavior between spouse's parents and children's spouses, and outright avoidance often characterizes the relationship between an individual and his spouse's parent of the opposite sex. After the marriage has endured for a few years and children have been born, these in-law relationships become more relaxed, taking on the characteristics of consanguineal ties.

Behavioral Variability

Although there is widespread general agreement as to the ideal forms that the relationships between different classes of kinsmen should take, there is much individual variation in specific cases. For, however much kinsmen may be sociologically allocated to various classes, the different kinsmen in a given class are perceived as individuals, each with his own personality, virtues, quirks, and foibles.

In practice there are two types of variation in kin–class behavioral patterns. In the first, an individual acts toward a kinsman in a way considered highly unconventional. One unmarried man with no siblings refused to make a joint swidden with his elderly widowed mother, with the result that both lost their crops because of insufficient guarding. This behavior on the part of the son was widely thought highly inappropriate. Another man threatened his first cousin with a knife in a gambling altercation and had to leave the village under a cloud of public disapproval. Both these cases exhibit behavior highly at variance with that which should normally be extended to these kinsmen, and both were regarded as exceptional cases by the rest of the community.

In the second type of variation, we find an individual behaving differentially toward two kinsmen of the same category. A person may have a much closer relationship with one mother's sister than with another, or may choose to join one sibling rather than another in building a new village house. Generally, an individual will have closer relations with kinsmen who belong to his residential groups, the *dangau* and *lewu'* families, than with kinsmen outside these groups. But even, say, within the same village household (*lewu'* family), there are often differential relationships among kinsmen of the same category. There is one *lewu'* family in Siong containing three married siblings in the second generation, each of whom is the focus for a different economically independent *dangau* family. The *dangau* families of two of the siblings show a high degree of cooperation, and usually work contiguous swidden plots. The *dangau* family of the third sibling is usually excluded from this close working relationship, and the general explanation tendered by the community at large is that this third sibling is not very industrious, fails to carry his own weight, and would tend to be a liability in a cooperative relationship.

Beyond the range of his residential groups, an individual will establish closer personal ties with some kinsmen of a particular category than with others. A boy who attends high school in a distant town will usually live with a sibling, cousin, uncle, aunt, or other kinsmen there, and establish with that kinsman an especially close personal relationship that will carry over into later life. In other cases, differential association patterns may be based on considerations of friendship or relative age. A young man planning to go diamond hunting in the north may prefer to take along one first cousin with whom he is especially friendly rather than another of comparable age.

In short, although many persons are recognized as kinsmen, and kin terms of address are extended to others, the behavior patterns which ideally regulate relations between different classes of kinsmen are in fact effectuated selectively as individual dyadic ties.

9

The Dangau Family

THE MOST IMPORTANT PADJU EPAT KIN GROUP is the *dangau* family, which can be considered the basic structural unit in Padju Epat society. A residential group whose characteristic locus is a swidden house (*dangau*), the *dangau* family forms a primary production and consumption unit in the economic sphere. In the agricultural labor exchange system, it is the basic unit, and it acts as a group in fulfilling the formal kindred obligations of its members. It owns common property such as tools, weapons, rubber trees, field houses, and a distinctive strain of rice seed. Finally, each *dangau* family has a head who organizes the group's activities and acts as its representative or spokesman in extrafamilial affairs.

The Residential, Production, and Consumption Unit

The 564 people of Telang, Siong, and Murutuwu are distributed among 121 *dangau* families. The size of the *dangau* family in these villages ranges from one to ten persons with a mean of 4.68. In addition to its village domicile (*lewu'*), which it may share with other families, each *dangau* family maintains one or more field houses (*dangau*), which, as I have indicated earlier, may show considerable variation in size and quality. *Dangau* families that are farming two or more swidden plots will usually have a main field house of fairly substantial size, while maintaining only small huts, barely large enough to accommodate a single sleeping person, in the others. Even *dangau* families whose farms are located close to the village usually possess at least one substantial field house, for field houses provide more than shelter: they serve as a base for agricultural operations; as a storage place for tools and harvested rice; as a kitchen for preparing both family meals in the swidden and the food that must be served by hosts to workers in the cooperative labor exchange system; and as a primary rubber processing station by *dangau* families that are tapping nearby trees.

71

The residential pattern that a particular *dangau* family follows may vary considerably from year to year, depending on such factors as the number, distance, and size of swidden plots, the location of mature rubber trees, the proximity of neighbors, and the personal inclinations of family members.

With the exception of certain interfamilial cooperative activities that will be discussed below, each *dangau* family cultivates its own swidden plots independently. In order to minimize the chances of crop failure, many *dangau* families (50.4 percent in 1963–1964) maintain at least two, and sometimes more, swidden plots in a given agricultural year. The total area of swidden worked by a single *dangau* family during my stay ranged from .62 acre to 27.4 acres, with a mean of 5.66 acres. Only one *dangau* family, that of the sub-district officer's assistant, did not engage in agriculture.

About 50 percent of the total area cultivated in any growing season is first-year swidden, 30 percent second-year, and 15 percent third-year swidden, with the rest devoted to fourth and fifth-year plots. The majority of *dangau* families (75.2 percent) was cultivating at least one first-year swidden plot during the agricultural year of 1963–1964.

Leaving aside such factors as crop loss due to disease or animal destruction, the tremendous variability both in the quality of Padju Epat swidden plots and in the care with which they are planted and tended obviates any hypothetical correlation between total swidden area maintained and *dangau* family productivity. The yields reported from the plots of twenty-one Telang and Siong *dangau* families ranged from 1.26 to 40.02 bushels per acre of threshed but unhusked rice, with a mean yield of 10.3 bushels per acre.

However, for present purposes, it is less important to consider harvests in terms of yields per acre than to evaluate the adequacy of the rice harvest in meeting the annual consumption requirements of the various *dangau* families. A complex set of factors goes into each *dangau* family's calculation of its annual rice needs: the number and ages of its members, its accustomed standard of living, the food requirements for family-sponsored cooperative work activities, and the family's kin and other social obligations that call for occasional donations of rice. On the average, a family comprising two adults and three children requires about twenty-eight bushels of threshed rice per year.

There is no real correlation between the number of members in a *dangau* family and the total area of swidden it cultivates. One Siong *dangau* family of two members cultivated over fourteen acres, while a Telang *dangau* family of six farmed less than one acre. And, since much of the area in second and third-year swidden is devoted to mixed fruit and vegetable crops, many *dangau* families harvest rice in amounts considerably below their annual needs.

When I analyzed the 1964 harvest figures of twenty-one Telang and Siong *dangau* families, I found that three-quarters of them harvested considerably less rice than they required for the year. Of the *dangau* families that reaped an adequate harvest, all recorded fairly large surplusses ranging from 150 to 450 percent of their requirements. As a group, though, these twenty-one families harvested only 52 percent of their annual rice requirement. Thus it appeared that a good many of these families were going to have to buy rice, perhaps for a considerable time, before the next year's harvest was in.

It is important to keep in mind that some families in almost any society whose subsistence system is based on swidden agriculture will have deficiencies in any given year. Padju Epat offers no exception to this rule, but may experience somewhat greater shortages than do other Dayak groups that have been described in Sarawak. The poor quality of Padju Epat's soil may be primarily responsible for the relatively low productivity of the area's swidden plots, although other factors enter in. Whatever the causes, it is apparent that many Padju Epat *dangau* families can expect periodic rice shortages and must be prepared to make up deficiencies through purchases. Thus, each *dangau* family must have some form of potential cash income that can be exploited when needed. Seasonal fruit sales, rattan cutting, canoe making, and various forms of artisan labor can bring in money on occasion, but by far the most important cash-producing activity available to local *dangau* families is rubber tapping.

Dangau Family Rubber Holdings

Over 80 percent of all *dangau* families in Telang and Siong own rubber trees, although only about 50 percent owned mature trees that were producing in 1964. The potential latex yield for Telang and Siong was about 1700 pounds per day, or about 620,000 pounds per year. Without going into all the complexities surrounding the marketing and pricing of the various grades of rubber produced in Padju Epat, suffice it to say that my calculations indicate that if the producing rubber trees of Telang and Siong were tapped to their full potential, the profit from rubber sales in these two villages would be equivalent to the purchase price of from 936 to 1,325 bushels of husked rice and would be more than sufficient to cover any expenditures for rice necessitated by the insufficient harvests of 1964.

Rubber trees, then, are a valuable asset to any *dangau* family that owns them. It must be stressed, however, that not every *dangau* family which owns mature rubber trees taps them all on a regular basis or works the trees themselves. Many tap their trees only when cash is needed. Some make their trees available to others, either kinsmen or nonkinsmen, to tap on a profit-sharing basis, so that even families that do not own productive trees may avail themselves of this economic resource.

The Padju Epater finds rubber cultivation a psychologically satisfying as well as remunerative mode of economic endeavor. Planting and maintenance are easy, and the tapping does not have to be performed with adherence to any set schedule. Tapping operations are begun or terminated as the rhythm of the *dangau* family's activities may dictate. Trees can be tapped during the less busy periods of the year and neglected whenever the family wishes to direct its attentions elsewhere. In a given year, a family may wish to tap only those rubber trees that are near its current base of swidden operations, so that its trees may either be tapped intermittently or contracted to some outsider. After tapping, the processed latex may be sold or stored until such time as the owners are moved to dispose of it. If the family is in a particularly strong financial bind, its trees may be sold, although this course of action is not lightly taken.

The Labor Exchange System

The *dangau* family forms a unit in an agricultural labor exchange system which operates on a small scale in swidden clearing operations and on a relatively larger scale in planting and harvesting activities. All *dangau* families participate in this "day for a day" exchange system, termed *panganrau*. Each man-day of work rendered by outsiders to a *dangau* family should, in time, be repaid to the workers' respective *dangau* families. The head of each *dangau* family must keep a mental reckoning of where its members have worked and which families have sent members to work on its own plots. In terms of credits and debts each individual is counted rather than the family as a unit. Thus if one *dangau* family sends three members to plant for another family, it is expected that the debt will be worked off by three members from the second family. All except younger children are considered equal in the system; work rendered by a man may be repaid by a woman or vice versa. Children are an ambiguous factor. Some families count them in the exchange system while others do not, and this occasionally leads to hard feelings. However, many children work just as hard as adults, and especially where such children represent underpopulated *dangau* families, they are quite acceptable.

A worker may also donate a day's labor that does not require any return. In such a case, the fact of the donation is made explicit to the host at the time the labor is performed. An individual might donate his labor for any one of several reasons, the most frequent of which were: as a service to an official, such as the district *adat* head or a schoolteacher; in order to get a free meal; or to attend a gay "party" affair. Unmarried youths often went where the pretty girls were and frequently donated their labor for the privilege.

The cooperative work groups that are formed for the heavy work of clearing are relatively small and fairly constant in membership. These groups usually consist of twelve to fifteen people from families that either live near each other in the village or maintain fields in fairly close proximity. The members of the clearing groups work in rotation on the plots of each participating family until the clearing and burning are completed. A host *dangau* family must furnish a full midday meal and a midafternoon snack to all those working in its plot.

Planting and harvesting groups are generally larger than the clearing groups and quite variable in membership. A day or so in advance, the head of a *dangau* family will announce that a particular plot is to be planted or harvested. In most instances, several plots in each village will be slated for work on the same day, so that there is a certain amount of competition for labor. The group working in a particular field may range in size from 10 or 20 to over 150 people, depending on the location of the plot, the number of people owing work to the host's family, the size of the family's active kindred, the popularity of the host, and the quality of food anticipated. A person wishing to assure a good turnout at his own plot will announce his intention to kill a pig for the midday meal. The work is usually interrupted by frequent rest breaks, and at least one and perhaps two or three meals will be served. Where only a small group appears, the work is hard and continues throughout the day with little feeling of gaiety. Where large crowds turn up, the actual work may be completed in an hour or two and the rest of the day spent in eating, gambling, and, on occasion, dancing.

The head of a *dangau* family will frequently deploy its members so that the family will be represented at two or three different cooperative agricultural activities on the same day. This practice helps the family maintain relationships with as many other *dangau* families as possible and indirectly serves to sustain community integration. The socially integrative aspect of the agricultural labor exchange system is clearly recognized by the Padju Epaters themselves. Some *dangau* families perform the bulk of their planting and har-

Participants at a cooperative rice planting.

vesting work by themselves, but then sponsor a special session in which feasting and relaxation are emphasized while actual work is kept to a minimum. It is generally conceded that the larger the group participating in a given activity, the lower will be the quality of the work performed. Human nature being what it is, Padju Epaters expect that an individual will take less care on another person's plot than on his own, an expectation that is fulfilled in actual practice. Where a great number of people are planting, the dibble holes are not optimally spaced, and much rice seed is wasted with either too little or too much going into each hole. Similarly, there is proportionally greater crop wastage when harvesting is performed by a large group than when it is accomplished by an individual *dangau* family. The festive atmosphere that surrounds most cooperative activities is certainly not conducive to careful work. It is fairly normal for a *dangau* family to plant part of its swidden area with fast maturing species of rice. This portion is usually sown by the *dangau* family itself, and cooperative labor groups are then employed for the planting of the slow maturing but high yielding varieties of rice that are the preferred crop. However, a few *dangau* families that place a premium on the careful, if laborious, planting and harvesting practices that provide maximum rice yields, will perform practically all the work on their respective swidden areas without help. But such families, who remain in the distinct minority because of the drudging labor involved, will usually discharge their social obligations to the community by sponsoring a token planting or harvesting session featuring an inviting menu and a modicum of work. Most Padju Epat *dangau* families either participate fully in the agricultural exchange system or else indicate their social good will by sponsoring a party session.

One Siong *dangau* family proved an exception to this general rule. The head of this family was a noted misanthrope who kept his family in a state of social isolation in which all agricultural work was carried out without cooperative assistance. The members of this family worked extremely hard and, it should be admitted, received extremely good returns for their labor.

In general, *dangau* families that contemplate sponsoring large planting sessions will wait until late in the planting season so that their members will have had time to build up enough labor exchange credits to ensure a large turnout at their cooperative sessions. A large *dangau* family is able to send three or four members out every day to acquire credits, while keeping several at home to plant fast maturing rice on its own fields. Smaller families cannot afford this diversification of effort, and will usually hold their cooperative planting sessions early in the season. Thus, the early part of the season is usually devoted to small plantings, with a gradual build-up to the large "party" plantings at the end of the season.

In the 1963–1964 agricultural season, I kept fairly careful attendance records at cooperative planting sessions in Telang and Siong. About 85 to 90 percent of all labor debts contracted in the cooperative exchange had been repaid by the end of the planting season. Most *dangau* families still owed one or two days of labor when the season was completed, but this was considered normal, given the complexity of the system. One *dangau* family, consisting of an elderly woman and her thirty-year-old simple-minded son, was still owed twelve days of labor at the completion of the planting season. Although he was a hard worker, a number of *dangau* families did not feel obliged to repay labor that had been contributed by the son, thus working a great hardship on the family in question. Many sympathetic villagers said that this attitude was not right, but there was little that could be done about it. Two Siong *dangau* families seemed to have more than their share of unpaid debts, a supposition verified by several informants. When I asked villagers what sort of sanctions might be invoked against these offenders, I was told that although such behavior might be tolerated for a year or two in the interests of community harmony, eventually their "creditors" would cease attending cooperative activities sponsored by the delinquent families.

The Dangau Family as a Ritual Unit

The *dangau* family sponsors life crisis, agricultural, and certain other ceremonies for its members. In the life crisis series, the *dangau* family conducts ceremonies to ensure safe childbirth, to mark the birth and naming of new babies, to celebrate the marriages of its members, and, finally, to perform death rites for its deceased members.

Life crisis ceremonies are usually held at the village house of the sponsoring *dangau* family. On such occasions, other villagers are invited to attend, and they must be fed a meal. The number of guests and the magnitude of the meal are governed by the nature of the ceremony and the importance attached to it by its sponsors. In general, the older the individual at the focus of the ceremony, the larger the crowd attracted and the better the meal served.

In contrast to the larger life crisis ceremonies, each *dangau* family also conducts a number of small ceremonies in connection with the agricultural cycle. Before the clearing of a new swidden plot begins, the senior male of the family should determine the suitability of the plot for rice cultivation by looking for favorable omens. At planting time, a woman sprinkles the family's rice seed with the blood of an animal to assure its germination. Christian families substitute a prayer for blood sprinkling in this ceremony. When the rice plants first begin to bud, women perform a cleansing ceremony in which water and coconut milk are sprinkled around the swidden plot to ensure a good harvest and protect the ripening grain from spirit and animal spoliation. All these rituals are small affairs, conducted in the swidden plots by members of the family. After the harvest and before any new rice may be eaten, each *dangau* family must perform a thanksgiving ceremony in their village house to mark the traditional beginning of the new year. Guests are invited to witness the rite and partake of a meal featuring the new rice. The various agricultural ceremonies do not require the services of a specialist; any competent adult who knows the proper ritual may officiate, although some are more appropriately conducted by individuals of a particular sex.

There are some ceremonies in which several *dangau* families may participate. Such jointly sponsored rituals may have a *lewu'* family base, as when a family ancestral spirit (*nanyu'*) is honored; a *tambak* group base, as in the *idjambe* cremation ceremony; a neighborhood base, as when several *dangau* families join together to celebrate the first rice ceremony; or even a "shaman base," as in the annual festival in which shamans feed their familiar spirits.

Dangau Family Property

Each *dangau* family possesses some property for the exclusive use of its members. This property normally includes durable agricultural, hunting, and fishing equipment, the family's swidden houses and rice storage bins as well as household goods such as cooking equipment, eating utensils, furniture, mosquito nets, sleeping mats, and bedding. A number of Padju Epat's *dangau* families owned Singer sewing machines, two owned battery operated radios, and one an ancient spring-driven phonograph. Most *dangau* families had canoes and a good many owned bicycles as well. Almost every *dangau* family had at least a few lengths of expensive batik or other decorated cloth to be worn by its women on special occasions or to be used as ceremonial decorations when needed. A family may also own some jewelry and other ornamental regalia that has either been inherited or acquired by its members in other ways.

Most *dangau* families, as I have already indicated, now own rubber trees, the proceeds of which flow into the family's exchequer. If an unmarried youth is tapping the family's trees, he is usually allowed to keep a certain amount of the profit for his personal use, but most of the money is supposed to be turned over to the family. However, it is not exceptional for a man, young or old, to gamble away on market day the entire proceeds from the rubber he has just sold.

To the sphere of individual property belong items of clothing, machetes and war swords for the men, some items of jewelry and other personal adornment including the wrist watches, operative or not, that many men possess. Whatever a *dangau* family member makes or earns through his own individual effort is considered his personal property. Thus, a youth who makes a canoe by himself and sells it can keep the proceeds for his own uses. Similarly, women may sell baskets, mats, or vegetables at market to earn a little cash. However, the luxury of calculating finances separately is only possible for unmarried persons, for adults with families contribute their cash earnings to the family treasury.

The Sacred Rice Strain

Almost every Padju Epat *dangau* family possesses a unique strain of sacred rice that serves as the local home of the rice spirit. This sacred rice is the focus of annual propitiative rituals that are conducted by the *dangau* family to ensure the good will of the rice spirit, upon which the family's well being depends. Each year, a tiny circular portion of the family's main swidden plot is set aside for the cultivation of sacred rice. After harvesting and threshing, it is kept in a special bark container. Although it may be eaten on special ritual occasions, the sacred strain should never be allowed to run out, for there must always be enough left to be planted the following year.

A few years after the marriage of a couple, when they appear to have formed a stable union, a special agricultural ceremony called a seed marriage is performed on their behalf. For this ceremony, the natal *dangau* families of each spouse contribute small amounts of their own strains of sacred rice. The two stocks of sacred rice are mixed together in the course of the seed marriage ceremony, thereby producing a new and unique strain of sacred rice specific to the new *dangau* family.

Dangau Family Spokesman

One member of each *dangau* family is recognized as its head, or perhaps more appropriately, as its spokesman, since his function is more to represent the family in dealings with outsiders than to regulate the family's internal affairs. The senior adult male member of the *dangau* family usually serves as its spokesman. A woman may act as spokesman, but ordinarily does so only when there is no responsible adult male resident in the family. Women may also serve in this capacity on a temporary basis during the absence of the family's regular spokesman. Only 10 (8.3 percent) of the 121 *dangau* families of Telang, Siong, and Murutuwu had women serving as spokesmen.

The responsibilities of *dangau* family spokesman are fairly diffuse. In general, he represents the *dangau* family in all formal dealings with outsiders. This may include participation in the planning and performance of jointly sponsored ceremonies, and representation of the *dangau* family in *adat* legal cases or in the formal negotiation of marriage contracts. He is also considered the legal representative of the family by the national bureaucracy, and is held responsible for the payment of the family's taxes and for the fulfillment of any other obligations stipulated by law or administrative regulations.

Within the bosom of the family, the influence wielded by the spokesman depends on the quality of the dyadic relationships that he maintains with the rest of its members. As the senior male in most families, he usually enjoys a position of dominant leadership, but as in many other societies, Padju Epat has its share of henpecked husbands and domineering wives, abused parents and willful children. In some *dangau* families the spokesman makes all important decisions, paying little attention to dissenting opinions from other family members, while in others he plays the role of consensus architect.

Structural Phases in the Life of the Dangau Family

The membership of a *dangau* family is not static, but shifts over time as it passes through the various stages of what might be considered a corporate life cycle. The *dangau* family's life cycle roughly parallels that of the husband and wife who serve as its focus; it is born when the focal couple first begins to act as an independent economic unit, reaches maturity with the advent of children, passes through a declining middle age as children secede after marriage, and dies with the focal couple or with the absorption of a surviving spouse into the *dangau* family of a married child.

The general stages through which the vast majority of *dangau* families pass may be technically termed: incomplete nuclear (a husband and wife with no children), complete nuclear (a husband and wife plus their unmarried children), complete stem (a husband, wife, and their unmarried children plus one married child and the latter's spouse and children), reduced nuclear (a husband and wife alone, all children having seceded after marriage), and broken stem (a husband and wife, a single aged parent of one of the spouses, plus the couple's children).

A couple may commence its married life either as dependent members in a complete stem *dangau* family, or as the focal couple in an independent *dangau* family of the incomplete nuclear type. A major provision of the *adat* legal code stipulates that a newly married couple should live with the bride's family for five years while the husband performs "bride service" for his wife's parents. However, minor provisions of the *adat* code permit the period of bride service to be reduced or eliminated by the payment of specified ritual fines to the bride's family. The ideal of initial uxorilocal residence is still realized in the majority of today's marriages. Thus, in the initial stage following marriage, a newly wed couple has two options: they may spend a few years as dependent members within the natal *dangau* family of one of the spouses, generally that of the wife, or they may immediately establish themselves as the focus of a new, independent *dangau* family. In 1964, about 12 percent of Padju Epat's *dangau* families were at the complete stem stage, while only 2 percent were at the incomplete nuclear stage.

After marriage, children are usually not long in coming, and a couple that has taken up initial uxorilocal residence generally has at least one child before they attain independent *dangau* family status. If the wife proves barren (11 percent of Padju Epat's married women over forty years in age had been childless) or if all children die in infancy, children are usually adopted from the families of close kinsmen. Independent and with children, individual *dangau* families spend the greater part of their corporate lives at the complete nuclear stage. About 50 percent of Padju Epat's *dangau* families were in this stage when I was living in the area.

As their children mature, a focal couple's *dangau* family may pass through the complete stem stage if a child and his spouse remain as dependent members after their marriage. The complete stem stage is only a temporary configuration, for within a few years the junior couple will secede from the parental family to establish its own independent nuclear *dangau* family. Ideally, the conjugal family of the first or older child of the senior couple automatically secedes when a subsequent child marries and remains in the parental *dangau* family. This pattern seems to be realized in actuality, since my census data revealed no *dangau* families containing more than one married sibling in the junior generation. As indicated above, about 12 percent of the district's *dangau* families were in the complete stem stage.

The composition of the *dangau* family may alternate between complete nuclear and complete stem until all children have married and seceded. When only the focal couple, now rather old, remain, the *dangau* family has reached the reduced nuclear stage. The spirit of *dangau* family autonomy is very strong among Padju Epaters, and older people will try to maintain their economic independence as long as possible. For these older people, the alternative to autonomy is absorption into another *dangau* family that can provide for their needs. As long as the husband and wife both survive, their *dangau* family is viable, provided certain conditions are met. After all their children have married and seceded from their *dangau* family, an old couple is in a position to remain independent as long as their health is good and they can call on the assistance of close kinsmen to aid them in the execution of the more taxing subsistence tasks that become increasingly burdensome with their advancing years. Participation in the normal labor exchange system assures the old couple of assistance in accomplishing the more arduous agricultural chores connected with clearing, planting, and harvesting. For the rest, a hard working couple might be able to make out by itself, although more usually it should be possible to get help from juvenile kinsmen, especially grandchildren, belonging to the *dangau* families of close kinsmen. These latter *dangau* families, for their part, can usually afford to relinquish the occasional services of one or two suitably aged children to assist elderly relatives in reduced nuclear *dangau* families. The viability of this unit is attested by the fact that 11 percent of all Padju Epat's *dangau* families were of the reduced nuclear type. In fact, there were no *dangau* families in the district which contained an absorbed old couple.

In the preceding chapter I remarked on the quality of the grandparent–grandchild relationship and the role of grandchildren in providing a form of social security for their grandparents. In some cases, a grandchild or great grandchild may actually take up full-time residence with an old couple, producing a "reduced nuclear with grandchildren" configuration that has most of the attributes of a complete nuclear *dangau* family. Five percent of the district's *dangau* families were of this type, which generally occurs where the members of a reduced nuclear *dangau* family have no close relatives of suitable age resident in the same village but who do have one or more grandchildren who could take up residence with them. In such a situation, the old couple's children are under an obligation to send one or more of their own children back to look after the old folks. All of the children of one old Telang couple were living outside the Padju Epat region. One of their sons, an Army man stationed at the western end of the province, dispatched two of his boys to Telang to help his parents and keep them company. Similarly, there was another old Telang couple who had no suitably aged close kinsmen living in the village. Their son, who had followed his wife in marriage to Murutuwu, sent his own son back to Telang to live with the old couple.

In some cases, an otherwise viable reduced nuclear *dangau* family will evolve into one of the "reduced nuclear with grandchildren" type through the absorption of grandchildren from families broken by death or divorce. A Muru-tuwu couple with a number of children and grandchildren living in the vicinity had been operating as a reduced nuclear *dangau* family for some years. In 1960, one of their daughters and her husband died in quick succession, leaving behind four children. Three of the orphans were then absorbed into the *dangau* family of the old couple. A Siong widower with a nine-year-old daughter remarried and settled with his new wife in an emigre village to the north. The daughter, who did not get on too well with her stepmother, was eventually sent back to Siong to live with her paternal grandparents, by whom she was heartily welcomed.

A *dangau* family is generally rendered inviable when one of the spouses in the reduced nuclear family dies. The surviving spouse is usually absorbed into the *dangau* family of a married child as a dependent member. This fusion creates a broken stem *dangau* family, a developmental stage represented by about 12 percent of Padju Epat's *dangau* families. If the absorbed surviving spouse is a woman, the broken stem configuration is a relatively stable one that will continue until her death. However, if the survivor is a man, the broken stem configuration is generally unstable and will probably break up, with the old man remarrying and establishing a new independent nuclear *dangau* family. In thirteen of the fourteen extant broken stem *dangau* families in my sample, the old person was a woman.

There are two reasons for the differential stability of these two configurations. First, female survivors of reduced nuclear families are more readily accepted than males into the *dangau* families of their children. Even the oldest women are capable of performing the niggling, recurrent, day-to-day tasks that fall to the female lot: cooking, cleaning up, washing clothes, weeding, making baskets, and tending babies. Thus, industrious widowed or divorced women are usually accepted with alacrity into a *dangau* family, especially by its female members, who can expect to have their own work loads reduced somewhat. On the other hand, the older a man becomes, the less capable he gets of carrying out the specialized heavier tasks allocated to him in the sexual division of labor. Old men are usually considered burdens who contribute little but who must be looked after, cooked and washed for, and otherwise catered to. Here, the burden falls most heavily on the women of the family, who contend, usually rightly, that they are kept busy enough serving the needs of their own families of procreation without taking on any additional responsibilities. Just as "only a mother can love an ugly child," so too Padju Epaters feel that only a wife can be expected to look after the everyday needs of an old man with any degree of zealousness. Thus, it behooves a widower or divorcé, even in his sixties, to remarry as soon as possible, and pressure to do so is brought on him by kinsmen, and indirectly from the ladies of the family. Such pressure is not put on old women.

Secondly, there is a universally expressed and observed cultural proscription that women should not marry men younger than themselves. A man, on the other hand, may marry as young a woman as he can find to accept him.

When they want or need to remarry, older widowers and divorcés can generally find younger wives. However, the opportunities for women to remarry decline with increasing age as the pool of older men becomes steadily reduced. Thus, older widows have neither the opportunities nor the pressures to remarry, while old widowers have both.

There are a few other types of *dangau* family configurations. Although represented in about 8 percent of Padju Epat's *dangau* families, these are generally temporary configurations generated by divorce, and their characteristics are too variable to allow summarization in a work of this kind. Suffice it to say that the *dangau* family is a dynamic kin group whose structural features and personnel change in patterned ways over time.

10

The Bumuh

THE BUMUH IS A KIN GROUP comprising all the descendants of an individual, who can be termed its progenitor or focal ancestor. Each *bumuh* was associated with an estate, transmitted from its focal ancestor, in which its members shared rights. Theoretically, the estate could not be divided, so that its members inherited only the right to use *bumuh* property. The estate could comprise land-use rights, fruit trees, houses, and various sorts of heirloom property such as gongs, old weapons, Chinese ceramic wares, and ritual paraphernalia. Not all *bumuh* estates contain the complete range of property listed above, and some have very little at all. Although all the members of a *bumuh* have rights in its estate, not all have an equal opportunity to exercise these rights. The mechanisms mediating the differential access of its members to the *bumuh* estate are discussed below.

In each succeeding generation, one member of the *bumuh* serves as custodian of its estate. It is the duty of the custodian to look after the estate and to convene the other members of the group whenever a matter affecting the *bumuh* or its estate must be decided. Following these introductory remarks, a more detailed description will be presented of the relationship between the *bumuh* and its estate, considering first the question of land rights.

Land Rights

In any agricultural society, institutionalized means must be provided for regulating the allocation of arable land to its members. In Padju Epat, although the village community as a corporate group traditionally exercised ultimate ownership of the land within its boundaries, in practice, the use rights to particular forest areas were vested in descent groups. According to the principles of the Padju Epat *adat* legal system, the right to farm a particular area within the village territory is initially secured by the individual that first clears it from virgin forest. Thereafter, that individual has exclusive rights to farm the area. Such an individual might be termed a "pioneer" and the use rights so obtained called "pioneer use rights."

Upon the death of a pioneer, the right to cut swiddens in areas where he had established pioneer use rights devolved upon his sons and daughters and other bilineal descendants, although as I shall explain, not all of these descendants inherited use rights of equal strength. Thus, the pioneer could be seen as the progenitor of a *bumuh* descent group, and the land to which he had established pioneer use rights became part of the estate associated with that *bumuh*.

As the children of a pioneer grew up, married, and seceded one by one from his *dangau* family, some remained affiliated with the parental village household as members of a larger *lewu'* family, while others "followed" their spouses in marriage to become affiliated with the *lewu'* families of those spouses. For the discussion that follows, it will be useful to describe the state of maintaining affiliation with the parental or natal *lewu'* family after marriage as "endofiliation," and that of establishing post-marital affiliation with the *lewu'* family of a spouse as "exofiliation." The locus of post-marital affiliation is ordinarily clearly established at the time of an individual's marriage.

Of the children of the pioneer, one, either male or female, that had married endofiliatively was designated to serve as custodian of the estate and spokesman for the *bumuh*. At the present time, the custodianship generally passes to the head of the village household in which the former custodian had resided, the rationale expressed by current Padju Epaters being that the proper successor to the custodianship was the individual who had taken care of the former custodian in his old age. As stated, the custodian may be either a man or a woman, although in the cases that I have recorded, men considerably outnumber women.

As custodian succeeds custodian, an identifiable descent line emerges at the center of the bilineal *bumuh*. Padju Epaters call such a succession line a *tutur*, a term that may be applied to any important line of succession. Thus, *tutur* are recognized and often memorized for a succession of office holders such as the *tutur* of village or *adat* heads; the *tutur* of recognized shamans of a particular type; the *tutur* of owners of a valuable war sword; or of the owners of a spirit tree. With the passage of generations the pioneer's descendants lose track of the *bumuh* founder's identity and orient themselves to the *tutur* of custodians rather than to the group's progenitor. Thus, an individual wishing to demonstrate his right to *bumuh* membership need only prove his descent from a recognized custodian of the group.

A good memory is one of the practical prerequisites for filling the position of *bumuh* custodian, and each custodian is generally able to recite the names of his more recent predecessors in the *tutur* of custodians. The memory qualification is important too because the custodian of a *bumuh* is responsible for knowing the details of all legal transactions which affect the *bumuh* and its estate. It is his duty to memorize the inventory of estate property and any special traditions connected with individual items of it, as well as the terms of important marriage contracts and *adat* legal decisions.

I have mentioned that although the use rights established by a pioneer to various swidden sites are inherited by his bilineal descendants, not all descendants inherit rights of equal strength. The point of this observation can now be made a little clearer.

After his death, a pioneer's children who had contracted endofiliative marriages inherit the primary right to use the plots that he opened. His children who had married exofiliatively fall into two categories: those who had maintained postmarital residence within their natal village inherit a secondary right to use pioneer plots; those who had followed their spouses to another village inherit a tertiary right to the use of these plots.

For convenience I will refer to individuals inheriting primary, secondary, and tertiary rights in the estate of a *bumuh*, as being primary, secondary, and tertiary members respectively of that *bumuh*. However, this does not reflect any terminological categories recognized by the Padju Epaters themselves.

As the general principles relating to the inheritance of *bumuh* rights were explained to me by several Padju Epat *adat* experts, the children of a *bumuh*'s secondary members inherit tertiary use rights, while the children of tertiary members inherit only residual rights in the *bumuh* estate. Individuals inheriting only residual rights may be termed residual members of the *bumuh*.

The bases on which primary, secondary, and tertiary use rights are allocated to *bumuh* members closely resemble the ordering of degrees of responsibility that children have in caring for their aging parents. Those children who marry endofiliatively have the greatest responsibility; they inherit primary rights. Those who marry exofiliatively but within the natal village have lesser responsibility and inherit secondary rights. Those who marry outside their natal village have the least responsibility and inherit tertiary rights to the estate. Considering that the person who becomes custodian is the endofiliative child who has actually taken care of his parent, one may make a good case for the institutionalized close relationship between the inheritance of *bumuh* estate rights and a system of social security for the aged. Padju Epaters certainly see the relationship in this light.

A given *dangau* family will have rights of varying sorts in a large number of swidden plots. If the wife is the endofiliative spouse, she will have primary rights to some swidden plots mediated through her natal *lewu'* family, tertiary or residual rights to other plots inherited through her exofiliative parent, and residual rights in a large number of plots controlled by *bumuh* in which she is a residual member. Her exofiliative husband, on the other hand, will have secondary or tertiary rights to some plots mediated through his natal *lewu'* family, tertiary or residual rights to other plots inherited through his exofiliative parent, and also residual rights in a large number of other plots.

At the beginning of an agricultural season, members of a *dangau* family mentally review or actually survey the various sections of forest in which they have inherited use rights. One or two sections might be earmarked as suitable for clearing and marked by placing crossed sticks on trails adjacent to the selected spots. If the *dangau* family selects a plot to which none of its members have primary rights, the custodian of the *bumuh* estate holding rights to the land should be informed. The practical differences between primary, secondary, tertiary, and residual rights become apparent only when two individuals holding rights of a different degree claim the same swidden site. In such cases, the individual holding rights of a higher order has the dominant claim, and the other must withdraw from the site in question. If two claimants have identical rights, the case must be brought before the custodian, who may render any decision on the matter that he sees fit. The custodian himself has first choice on swidden sites whose rights are held by the *bumuh*.

If no one claiming rights to a particular piece of swidden land remains in the region, those rights may revert to the village corporation, in which ultimate land rights are vested. The village head has the power to grant the use of such reverted land to any villager who makes application. Such rights may be termed "reverted use rights."

Residual members of a *bumuh* theoretically may exercise their rights in its swidden land only if all recognized primary, secondary, and tertiary members of the *bumuh* have temporarily waived their rights or emigrated from the village. Traditionally, few residual members would have had the opportunity to exercise their rights. Good land was relatively scarce, especially in Telang and Siong. All the best sites would probably have been claimed by individuals with primary or secondary rights, whereas plots that could be obtained through the exercise of tertiary or residual rights would have been of poor quality. Most tertiary and residual members of any *bumuh* should have access to better plots through other *bumuh* in which they held primary or secondary memberships. However, since the pattern of wholesale emigration from Padju Epat began several generations ago, residual (and even reverted) rights have become somewhat more important.

The *bumuh* does not control specific, marked swidden plots, but rather rights to farm in certain general areas of the village territory. In secondary forest, it is troublesome to maintain boundary markers for swidden plots, and furthermore, an ancestor who established pioneer rights to an area probably cleared a number of contiguous plots in the course of several years. His descendants then inherit generalized rights over the whole area. Since nearly every square yard of Padju Epat territory has its own distinctive name, it is possible to distinguish different swidden areas with a fair amount of discrimination.

Trees

Within the forest, fruit trees rather than fences provide the points of reference for swidden rights. As part of life's normal routine, when a family is living at its swidden hut, the seeds and other inedible parts of fruit consumed are tossed nonchalantly out the doors and windows. Many of these seeds sprout, and before long a flourishing colony of fruit tree seedlings surrounds the hut. Some survive, and long after the hut has been abandoned, the trees continue to mark the site. When the spot is next cleared for swidden, mature fruit trees will not be felled, and in fact an *adat* fine must be paid to placate their spirits if the trees should accidentally be singed during the burning of a field. In time, the fruit trees, especially the majestic durian, come to soar over the forest *hoi polloi*, serving as beacons in the sea of trees. Such trees become part and parcel of the *bumuh* estate. When I was visiting friends in their swidden fields, and asked where their land rights came from, frequently one would point to some large fruit trees and say, "Those are the remains of my wife's grandfather's occupancy, and we get our rights from him."

In addition to serving as the focus for the assertion of land rights, produce from the fruit trees belongs to the *bumuh* estate. Individual descendants of the unwitting planter may help themselves to the fruit on a piecemeal basis at any time. If a member wants to harvest the entire crop of fruit, the *bumuh* custodian should be informed and all other people having rights in the tree or trees should be allowed the opportunity to join the project. The fruit is then split equally among the participating *dangau* families, while those who have rights in the trees but do not assist in the harvesting, receive none of the fruit. If it appears that no one with rights to a group of trees is going to pick the fruit, which frequently happens where trees are remotely located, with the custodian's permission, any member of the community may harvest the fruit himself. In such cases, it is customary to give the custodian 20 or 30 percent of the crop. This, of course, is the ideal arrangement. The unsanctioned purloinment of fruit is not unknown in Padju Epat. Since the Telang market does a thriving fruit export business during the appropriate season, fruit trees add a potential economic asset to the *bumuh*.

The estate in a few *bumuh* is increased by the possession of "canoe" and "bee" trees. Although most trees for Padju Epat's canoe industry grow in nonarable forest land in the public domain, some of the best trees have been purposely planted, becoming part of the estate property of the planter's descendants. After planting, the area around a canoe tree is kept clear so that the trunk will grow absolutely straight. Once it has gotten a good start, the tree can be left unattended, to be harvested several generations thereafter. Large canoes thirty to fifty feet in length can be carved from these trees. *Bumuh* members may use such trees for manufacturing canoes, or the custodian may sell them to nonmembers.

Another species of tall tree is very attractive to honey bees. Honey is much desired locally as a sweetening agent, and at various times individuals have planted "bee" trees. These trees, too, become *bumuh* property. One Murutuwu *dangau* family claimed to have rights in about thirty "bee" trees, although not all were then occupied. Bees sensibly prefer to nest at great heights, so that there is a certain amount of danger involved in honeying, at least for the individual who climbs the tree with a torch to burn out the bees. Thus the occasion of a honey harvest provides an opportunity for young men to exhibit their nerve and skill in tree climbing. As with harvesting of fruit, the collection of honey is a joint activity in which all *bumuh* members are invited to join. All those who participate share equally in the honey, with the exception that the tree climber may claim a larger share.

Personal Property

One type of valuable tree, the rubber tree, does not enter into the realm of the estate for transmission to the planter's *bumuh* descendants. Rubber trees are a straight commercial crop whose private ownership is unambiguously vested in the individual who plants them. When an individual wants to plant rubber trees on *bumuh* land, he should obtain the permission of the custodian, for the planting of rubber trees means, in effect, that no other member of the *bumuh* will be able to make use of that plot for fifty or more years. However, this latter point is a moot one, since most Padju Epaters now register their rubber lands with the government and thereby gain private title to them. In short, the effect of planting rubber on *bumuh* land is to withdraw it completely from the *adat* system that has traditionally governed land rights. Rubber trees, then, are private property that may be bought or sold without consulting anyone.

The property that an individual acquires during his own lifetime, either by exclusive inheritance or by dint of his personal efforts, may be transmitted as he sees fit. Before his death a man may dispose of his personal property by a simple announcement or, as frequently happens today, by written testament. He may decide for an equal division among his children, or favor one or two over the others. A large number of rubber trees that he has planted may be left to a child who has taken care of him in his old age, or he may pass on an heirloom war sword to that son who shows leadership capabilities or a special knowledge of *adat* law. A woman may will her special ritual paraphernalia to a daughter who has followed her as a practitioner of the shamanistic arts. Property that has been acquired jointly by a married couple will usually remain in the custody of the surviving spouse and be transmitted after the latter's death.

If a successful individual has acquired certain traditionally valued objects, such as bronze gongs, brass trays, or Chinese ceramic plates, he may choose to divide these, too, among his heirs on a piecemeal basis. However, a good collection of such prized objects is difficult to accumulate, and its possession gives the family status within the community. A person who has acquired such a collection for his family hates to see it dissipated through division; he may indicate that this part of his estate is not to be divided, but is to be held in common by his heirs. Such undivided property then becomes the joint heirloom property of the *bumuh* comprising his descendants.

Heirloom Property

The amount and quality of its heirloom property is one of the most important characteristics distinguishing one *bumuh* from another. Such property ideally consists of ancient gongs, spears, blowpipes, daggers, large Chinese jars incised with a dragon motive, ceramic plates, brass trays, cloth, antique clothing, plaited mats, assorted ritual paraphernalia, and other items of a more idiosyncratic character. There was tremendous disparity among *bumuh* with regard to their heirloom inventories.

Traditionally, most *bumuh* would possess a minimum of a few bronze gongs and brass trays that could be used by the family on ceremonial occasions. The execution of almost any traditional ceremony requires the presence of a few of these gongs and bowls. For important ceremonies much more is required in the way of equipment. For instance, the ritual attending a pre-burial ceremony prescribes the use of a number of large bronze gongs, brass bowls, brass pedestaled trays, and decorated cloths. If the bereaved household does not itself possess the required items, such equipment could be obtained from the *bumuh* estate of the endofiliative spouse; members of the family also were entitled to request the needed items from the custodians of the *bumuh* in which they held secondary, tertiary, and even residual rights. Necessary paraphernalia would be contributed for the occasion, provided there was not some other *bumuh* member with stronger rights who needed them for a ceremony of his own. Ordinarily the chances that two households within a *bumuh* would want the same equipment at one time were rather low, but when an important ceremony involving many families at once, such as the *idjambe* cremation ceremony, was held, the strain on a village's heirloom resources becomes acute. Some families, consequently, would have to scrape along with the bare minimum of ritual items that they themselves controlled.

The Tambak Group

THE TAMBAK GROUP IS A DESCENT GROUP comprising a founder, his endo-filiative descendants, and their spouses; each is associated with a particular ironwood receptacle (*tambak*) that serves as the last resting place for the ashes of its members. Like the *bumuh*, the *tambak* group has a head or custodian. The custodianship of a *tambak* group is usually passed to a member of the previous custodian's household. Thus, with each *tambak* group there is one household that serves as the locus of its custodian descent line. This household also functions as the repository for the *tambak* group's heirloom property.

Tambak groups differ from *bumuh* in two significant ways: (1) each is named and thus has a greater sense of focus and permanency than do the general run of unnamed groups; (2) membership is "optative exclusive," which means that although an individual has a limited choice as to which *tambak* group he will affiliate with, he may not belong to more than one at a time. An individual first belongs to the *tambak* group of his natal *dangau* family; *tambak* group membership is often changed at the time of marriage. After death, there is no room for further choice, since his ashes must be interred in only one *tambak*. Formal arrangements are necessary for the establishment of a *tambak* group, so that there is never any doubt as to when a new group has been founded, although later there may be some question as to when one ceases to exist. And because the establishment of a new *tambak* entails great economic outlay, new *tambak* groups are not often formed. Consequently, at the time of my stay in Padju Epat, there were relatively few *tambak*. On my visits to village burial sites, I was able to count twenty-two ironwood boxes, but for all practical purposes the *tambak* groups associated with some of these were already defunct.

Apart from the Moslem sector of Telang, traditionally every household, every *dangau* family and every individual in Padju Epat was associated with one or another *tambak* group. Christians, of course, do not inter the

91

remains of their dead in *tambak*, and they theoretically dissociate themselves from certain *tambak*-oriented activities. At least one Christian, however, an elder of the Telang church, functioned as the custodian for a *tambak* group. Since all *tambak* groups possess heirloom property, and since most of this property has a real monetary value in today's world, Padju Epat Christians find nothing in the tenets of their religion to preclude their involvement in the secular activities of *tambak* groups. A number of Christians also acted as sponsors for the corpses of animist kinsmen in the Padju Epat *idjambe* cremation ceremonies of 1963; in this role they participated in many of the activities connected with the ceremony, although being reasonably careful to avoid rituals involving spattering the blood of a sacrificial animal (*pilah*).

A given individual's *tambak* affiliation generally depends on his village residence (*lewu'*), although there are many extenuating factors that may affect this. Before marriage he is a member of the *tambak* group of his natal *dangau* family, which I term his "natal *tambak* group." The spouse who "follows" in marriage, whether male or female, becomes nominally affiliated with the *tambak* group of his endofiliative spouse, which I will call his "affinal *tambak* group." If the inmarrying spouse dies without children, his ashes may be interred in either his affinal or natal *tambak*; there is no set rule. The final disposition of the ashes in such a case would be decided by the heads of the families and *tambak* groups involved, and, if necessary, by the adjudicating elders. If the couple had been married a long time, had been happy together, and the inmarrying spouse had gotten on well with his in-laws, his ashes might very well be entered into his affinal *tambak*. An individual with an unhappy marriage would certainly be returned to his natal *tambak*. Once children have been born, the inmarrying spouse generally maintains affiliation with his affinal *tambak* group. In a society where some individuals may go through marriage as many as ten times, the *tambak* group affiliation of children sometimes gets a little confused in principle, but, in the event of such a child's death, the special features of each individual case would be taken into account by the adjudicators. The system of *tambak* group affiliation is not, at any rate, a rigid one. In the vast majority of cases, there is no ambiguity as to which *tambak* will receive a given person's ashes, but in a few cases, one can never be quite sure until death has occurred and the whole situation been discussed by the interested parties.

Social Stratification and Clientship

Tambak groups were traditionally associated with a formal system of social stratification. As I have described in Chapter 3, *tambak* are situated in a traditional, ranked order within the village graveyard. When I tried to ascertain the nature of the strata represented by the *tambak* groups, information was scant and somewhat conflicting in nature. The picture that emerged from conversations with various villagers seemed to contain four classes: "nobles" (*bangsawan*), "warriors" (*panglima*), "common people" (*panganak rama'*), and "clients" or "slaves" (*walah*). Each *tambak* was ostensibly associated with one of these classes, but when I tried to correlate actual named *tambak* with their associated classes, I found that the common people had none peculiarly their own. The allocation of *tambak* indicated a three-class system consisting of nobles, warriors and clients. Members of the first two classes were free to run their own lives, while those of the third were in a dependent status.

Among the free classes, not all members of noble *tambak* groups were close to the family lines from which individuals were chosen to fill positions of political authority. Similarly, although the term *panglima* is used for a war leader, not all members of warrior *tambak* groups were actually war leaders. Rather, the various warrior *tambak* groups had been founded by war leaders and were noted for producing warriors in certain family lines. The common people, then, consisted of the noble and warrior *tambak* group members that were not close to its key family lines. Thus, each noble and warrior *tambak* group had its sector of common people. The common people were full independent members of the community, although they were obliged to bear arms defensively when necessary.

Clients, on the other hand, formed a dependent class whose members were satellites of free individuals or families. There were several types of client: the *urai* was a person who had become a debt slave; the *kawalek* was a prisoner taken in battle; the *walah* was a child of either *urai* or *kawalek*. I use the term client to include all three subtypes. The client did not necessarily lead an unhappy life, but he was not his own master. He was politically and economically dependent on the arrangements made for him by his patron family. He would be given a swidden to work, and he would probably be permitted to marry, but only at his patron's discretion. He was guaranteed protection and given a certain amount of minimal economic security, but he was also expected to work where, when, and in what capacity he was directed. Clientship or "slavery" of the type described here is known in many parts of Borneo and the Malay world. However, from the records of Dutch colonial administrators, it appears that Padju Epat clientship existed in a particularly mild form in the mid-nineteenth century. The Dutch officially abolished "slavery" in Borneo in 1892.

Despite its reputed mildness, indistinct but unmistakable reflections of clientship could still be discerned in Padju Epat in 1964. When I talked to villagers about their ancestry and natal *tambak* group affiliations, there was no doubt that the stigma of client ancestry was keenly felt by some.

The bones of clients were cremated, for otherwise their spirits would remain around the village to cause trouble. But according to traditional Padju Epat *adat*, the ashes of a person of client status could not be interred in a free class *tambak*. Prior to 1897, client ashes were placed in large earthen jars termed *kosi*. After slavery was abolished in 1892, the earthen *kosi* jar was replaced by conventional ironwood *tambak*. These were titled Kosi Ukir (*ukir* means "carved, incised"), the title reflecting the client origins of the *tambak* groups. The first Kosi Ukir *tambak* was established in Telang for the 1897 cremation ceremony.

As I have suggested, the possession of client status did not impose onerous burdens on the individual client. If he were ambitious, a client could become rich through industrious activity. According to my Padju Epat friends who would talk objectively about the subject, most clients were poor and un-ambitious. However, there were cases known of clients who, by dint of hard work, had managed to acquire considerable wealth. Such a person was not doomed to remain in client status; with the performance of a special and expensive cleansing ritual prescribed by the *adat* code, a client could be raised to free status. The *adat* code permitted a client to marry a person of nonclient status. If the cleansing ritual were performed at the time of the wedding, the client was raised to the *tambak* group of his or her spouse; if not, the free spouse fell to client status. According to the *adat* head of Murutuwu, such cleansing ceremonies were still being performed in that village in the 1940's. Other evidence, as well, points to the fact that client status or ancestry was still recognized in Padju Epat until quite recently.

Padju Epat *adat* specifies that during the nine days of *idjambe*, a resin torch be kept lit in the village ceremonial hall where the ritual is being held. The torch should be tended by villagers of client status, for it was believed that the spirits of the clients being cremated would become the torch bearers and porters of the free spirits on their long journey to Datu Tundjung, the land of the dead. In the afterworld, the clients would continue to serve their free spirit masters.

When *idjambe* was held in Balawa in 1951, the ceremony is reported to have been rocked by a terrible row over the impressment as torch tenders of people with client origins. Balawans of client ancestry were said to be turning increasingly to the *mia* type of final death ceremony, mentioned in an earlier chapter, that does not involve cremation or *tambak*. By 1963, when *idjambe* was held in Murutuwu, Siong, and Balawa, an explicit policy had been estab-lished whereby the torch was to be serviced without regard to putative class associations. The people of Balawa, in fact, went so far in 1963 as to abolish all formal distinctions between *tambak* groups by combining the village's tra-ditional five *tambak* into one new "cooperative" *tambak*. The Balawans stated that this action was taken in the interests both of promoting community har-mony and of more closely adhering to the democratic principles of the mod-ern Indonesian state.

By the time of my arrival in Padju Epat in 1963, it appeared that all individuals who had been born into client *tambak* groups had either converted to Christianity or had acquired membership in other *tambak* groups through marriage. Although client *tambak* groups have ceased to function through loss of members, the memory of client ancestry lives on to rankle in the minds of some people. Understandably enough, these people were extremely reluctant to discuss their client connections. In the course of collecting family histories, I found that certain individuals, who otherwise had good memories in recalling lineal ancestors and their respective *tambak* group affiliations, suffered acute, though highly selective, genealogical amnesia when it came to some ancestors. Other people in a village knew who was of client descent, though they too were reluctant to discuss the matter. According to the *adat* legal system, it was a punishable offense to call a person a client who was not. Thus, whenever questions were asked about specific individuals of client descent or cases involving client marriages, all Padju Epaters were tight-lipped and reticent. Under the circumstances, it was impossible to get at the full operation and significance of the client institution as it once existed in Padju Epat.

Tambak Groups, Persistent and Ephemeral

The number of *tambak* groups is not fixed and unalterable. New ones have been formed while old ones disappeared. The establishment of a new *tambak* group symbolizes its founder's having attained an almost unique economic and social status. If the founder, either a man or a woman, feels that his personal status has reached such heights that he wishes to dissociate himself from his natal *tambak* group, he commissions the construction of a new *tambak* to serve as the repository for his own ashes and those of his bilineal descendants. On occasion, a new *tambak* group might be established for a person by his children after his death to do him honor. The new *tambak* is given a name, which is also applied to the *tambak* group associated with it. Telang's *tambak* Mas ("Golden Tambak") is an offshoot of an old noble *tambak* group. It was established in 1894 for Sota'ono, a former district chief of great renown, who was considered to be of such stature that there was not room enough in the old Telang graveyard to allow placement of his *tambak* at a suitable distance upstream from the older Telang *tambak*. Accordingly, *tambak* Mas was planted well upstream in a new *tambak* graveyard on the edge of the village.

Although there are now twenty-two *tambak* and associated *tambak* groups in Padju Epat, in the past there have been many others, now gone and forgotten. Over a long period of time, a core of *tambak* groups have demonstrated remarkable viability. Then, there have been other *tambak* groups that have enjoyed brief florescence while the memory of their founders' affluence lingered with the living, only to be abandoned when the costs of maintaining a separate *tambak* became too burdensome for its members. Sungking Siong was such an ephemeral *tambak* group, established about the turn of the century by a very rich man whose natal *tambak* group had been *tambak* Siong. His own ashes were placed inside the new *tambak*, but it was opened thereafter at only two *idjambe* ceremonies and then abandoned as his descendants returned to *tambak* Siong.

The factors militating against the survival of a new *tambak* group are primarily economic. The new group usually has few members, since it includes only the founder and his descendants who have not married into other *tambak* groups. At the time of cremation there are certain basic costs that each participating *tambak* group (each *tambak* group that has exhumed bones to be cremated) must bear, whether the group is cremating one person or fifty. As well as basic costs, there are additional minor costs for each corpse that are borne by the individual sponsoring families. Where a *tambak* group is cremating many corpses, the major expenses are shared among many families. If a *tambak* group is entering only a single corpse, which is often the case with a recently established *tambak*, the full weight of the basic expenses, as well as the added individual costs, will fall on a single family. Thus the social advantages of belonging to a distinctive *tambak* group may be more than offset by the concomitant economic disadvantages. Telang's *tambak* Damang Bola, founded by the man who had served as district *adat* head under Sota'ono, was last opened for *idjambe* in 1951. When one member of this *tambak* group was cremated in Murutuwu in 1963, the son of the deceased did not want to "open" the *tambak* all by himself, and thus "returned" his father's ashes to another *tambak*, named Ginun Rewau, from which Damang Bola had sprung. This is only one of the recent documented cases. In the past there must have been many similar, if unrecorded, births and deaths of *tambak* groups.

Tambak *group members butchering one of the pigs sacrificed during the cremation ceremony.*

12

The Lewu' Family

THE LEWU' FAMILY IS A KIN GROUP associated with the village house (*lewu'*) that serves to articulate individual *dangau* families with the more extensive *bumuh* and *tambak* groups. The builders of a village house become the founders of a *lewu'* family, and that house serves as the family's locus. The members of a *lewu'* family are its founders, their bilineal descendants, real or adopted, who have maintained post-marital affiliation with it, and the inmarrying spouses of the latter. In addition to its village house, the *lewu'* family owns heirloom property, controls primary rights to swidden lands, prescribes certain food taboos, and mediates *tambak* group affiliation. At any given time, a *lewu'* family will contain either one or several constituent *dangau* families who share in its property rights and, on occasion, act as a ritual unit. And, like the other kin groups already described, it has a head who acts as its spokesman and custodian of its property.

A village house might be built by a single individual, but because of the labor and cost involved, house construction was more usually a joint enterprise involving several closely related individuals, such as a set of siblings or a parent with several married children, who had all formerly been members of the same *lewu'* family.

Food Taboos

Most *lewu'* families are bound by certain food taboos. The members of one household may be prohibited from eating water buffalo meat, while to those of another, catfish might be taboo. Consumption of deer, mouse deer, and various types of birds, fish, and monkeys may also be forbidden to one or another household, although I could discover no household that could not eat pig, either wild or domesticated. In addition to household taboos that must be observed by all members of a *lewu'* family, there may be others that affect only individuals. Food prohibitions usually have their origin in illness. When a person becomes sick and a shaman is called in, the latter may diagnose that the spirit of a particular kind of food animal has caused the problem. Or it may be found that the bones of a certain animal affect a cure if rubbed on the patient. In either case, the patient is advised to abstain from eating that species of animal. Ordinarily, an individual's personal food taboos need not be observed by the other members of his household, unless a shaman has specifically stated that they should be. However, when an individual builds a new house, his food taboos come to govern the household, and the prohibited food may not even be brought into the house.

When an individual follows his spouse in marriage, he or she is no longer bound by the food restrictions of his natal household, but must observe those of the *lewu'* family of his endofiliative spouse. He will, however, continue to observe any personal food taboos.

The Lewu' Family as a Ritual Unit

The *lewu'* family acts as a ritual unit in the performance of certain spirit propitiation ceremonies, the most important of which is the annual post-harvest ceremony *mira ka'ayat*. In the course of this ceremony, various spirits are fed: the crocodile spirit Dewata, various animal spirits, the spirits of inanimate objects, such as large trees, and most important, the returned spirits of certain ancestors, termed *nanyu'*.

During an individual's lifetime, his body is inhabited by a life-giving spirit termed *amirue*. The *amirue* can leave the body during sleep, which occurs when an individual dreams. During sickness, a person's spirit is in a state of flux, constantly coming and going. While never leaving the body for too long a period, it flits in and out, unwilling to stay put. In this situation, a shaman will be called in to diagnose the sickness and to try to coax the spirit back into the patient's body on a permanent basis. However, if the shaman fails and the spirit does not want to return to the body, life cannot be long sustained. Shortly before death ensues, the *amirue* returns one last time and makes itself visible to the dying person in a form called *karama*. The appearance of the *karama* is the harbinger of death, and nothing can save the patient. After death, a deceased person's spirit is known as *adiau* until its arrival in the afterworld, whither it is conveyed by the ritual of the *idjambe* cremation ceremony. According to Padju Epat tradition, not all *adiau* are satisfied to remain in the afterworld; a few have an itch to return to Padju Epat to look after their living descendants. Through a dream or some other special sign such a spirit will inform the living world of its desire to return; the spirit will often direct that a suitable habitation be prepared. The returned ancestral spirit is termed *nanyu'*.

Usually a spirit house is prepared for the accommodation of the spirit, although *nanyu'* have been known to take up residence in stones or planks. Whatever the abode of the *nanyu'*, it is kept in the rafters of his former village house. Thus the spirit always lives above his progeny, giving a sheltering, all-embracing type of protection. Once ensconced in his new home, the *nanyu'* will look after such endofiliative descendants as continue to honor him by offering him food once a year during the *mira ka'ayat* ceremony. I have already mentioned that, in the absence of village guardian statues, the inhabitants of Padju Epat emigre settlements received their most important spiritual protection from the *nanyu'* lodged in their home villages.

Not every house in Padju Epat had a resident *nanyu'*. An old house which was the residence of the custodian of a *tambak* group or an important *bumuh* might have several *nanyu'*, while a new house might have none. For, occasionally, some members of an old, established *lewu'* family would secede from it to build a new house which would serve as the locus of a new, derivative *lewu'* family. The new family would have no *nanyu'* of its own and would usually join with the members of the older *lewu'* family for the celebration of *mira ka'ayat*. However, joint ceremonial arrangements of this type should be considered in the broader context of *lewu'* family growth and segmentation.

Lewu' Family Segmentation

In the course of forty or fifty years, a *lewu'* family would grow to comprise a fairly large number of constituent *dangau* families spanning three or more generations. A Padju Epat friend described for me the Murutuwu *lewu'* family that he belonged to as a child. The founder of this family had been Batur, a former Murutuwu village head and the great grandfather of my friend. Batur's house had been extremely large; prior to World War II it had been a bustling place, at least during certain seasons of the year. Twelve or thirteen *dangau* families were more or less full time residents, and perhaps another twenty, who farmed in emigre communities to the north, would return to the home village each year after the harvest was in. The house contained a number of rooms, in which each family could lock up its possessions when it left the village. My friend said that this large *lewu'* family formed a very warm, active and lively group that promoted close affective relationships among its members. Although each constituent *dangau* family remained economically independent, the families staying in the house at any one time would prepare and eat their meals together. The common eating arrangement made it possible for a few lazy members of the household to subsist on the contributions of other *dangau* families. This was apparently accepted with a fair amount of equanimity by the more productive *dangau* families since rice harvests were very good during this period, and Murutuwans claim that there was rarely a deficit. However, after World War II, economic conditions got worse, rice harvest surplusses declined, and most of the constituent *dangau* families of Batur's household emigrated up-country. Today the village house built on the same site accommodates only two *dangau* families.

Although each *dangau* family in a *lewu'* family was economically independent, the members of lower generations had to show deference to and accept advice from those of higher generation. Sometimes this chafed the younger, or perhaps older members might object to the way the *lewu'* family's custodian was running its affairs. In the normal routine constituent *dangau* families spend much of the year living in their individual swidden houses, and this must have done much to minimize the personal antagonisms that can build up in an extended family household. Over the years, some tensions must have developed. The occasion for the rebuilding of an old house presented an ideal opportunity for the establishment of new *lewu'* family configurations. Those who were happy with the old arrangement would work together with the head of the *lewu'* family to build a new house on the old site, while those who wished more independence were free to construct new houses on other sites, either individually or in partnership with other members of the old household.

It was the right of the *lewu'* family head to make use of the old house site for the construction of a new house. This new house formed the locus for a *lewu'* family that was the successor of the old *lewu'* family. I find it useful to term this group the "originative *lewu'* family." The other houses built by *dangau* families not maintaining membership in the originative *lewu'* family become the loci of new *lewu'* families which I term "derivative *lewu'* families."

In Murutuwu there was a large old house that was the locus of a *lewu'* family comprising ten *dangau* families. Seven of these *dangau* families were living in emigre villages and were not exercising their rights in the *lewu'* family. Of the other three *dangau* families who continued to live in the house, the husband in one and the wives in the other two were siblings. In 1959 the old house was thought too decrepit for further occupancy and was torn down. At that time the families of the three siblings decided to split up, and they built three houses close together. The three families got on very well together, but said that they liked the relative privacy that living in separate houses gave them. In addition, they felt that it was more modern to live in smaller houses. The values of privacy and modernity were frequently cited by Padju Epaters to account for the trend to smaller, less complex households.

Any ancestral spirit houses that had been present in the old house would be maintained in the new house of the originative *lewu'* family. The members of the derivative *lewu'* families would then join with the originative *lewu'* family in celebrating *mira ka'ayat* until the former had acquired ancestral spirits of their own.

The derivative *lewu'* families usually received a portion of the old *lewu'* family's heirloom property at the time of segmentation, although the details of the apportionment were subject to negotiation. If the custodian of a *tambak* group were a member of the old *lewu'* family, the *tambak* group heirloom property under his control would not be divided, but would be maintained in the house where the custodian resided.

Thus, segmentation may take place when the village house locus of a *lewu'* family is torn down. It is also possible at times other than the rebuilding of a house for one or more constituent *dangau* families to split off from the *lewu'* family to establish a new *lewu'* family. The head of the withdrawing *dangau* family would make known his intention of building a new house and request that he be given a division of the *lewu'* family's heirloom property. The request would be considered by the *lewu'* family head in consultation with the other members of the *lewu'* family. If for some reason it is decided not to give a share to the departing *dangau* family, then the latter simply withdraws to build a new house, but continues to derive its use rights to swidden land and estate property as if it were still resident in the originative *lewu'* family.

There are many factors that could lead a *dangau* family to dissociate itself from an originative *lewu'* family in this way. The house of the *lewu'* family might be too crowded so that some of the constituent *dangau* families had no place to store their personal belongings. The members of one *dangau* family might find themselves in conflict with other members of the *lewu'* family.

When I was living in Padju Epat, one Siong household was in the process of segmenting. In this case, a religious difference appeared to be the precipitating factor. This *lewu'* family contained four *dangau* families, one in the senior generation, and three based on a sibling set in the junior generation. Sometime before my arrival in the area, the members of two of the junior families had converted to Christianity, while the other two families remained animist. A certain estrangement developed between the Christian and animist components of the family. If an animist ceremony were held, the Christian members were reluctant to participate, because animal blood would be involved in purification. When a Christian ceremony was held, the *dangau* family of the animist parents would not attend. Once, when I attended a Christian naming ceremony in the house of this *lewu'* family, the baby's animist grandparents stayed out in their swidden and did not even come into the village. Shortly before my appearance in Padju Epat, the two Christian *dangau* families decided to secede from the parental household and jointly built a new house near Telang's market area. They postponed moving into the new house temporarily, and decided to rent it to the visiting anthropologist. They did move into the new house on the day that I took my final departure from Padju Epat. In this particular case, there was no request made to divide the *lewu'* family's heirloom property, which was considerable. The seceding *dangau* families' primary use rights to swidden plots and heirloom property continued to be mediated through the parental, originative *lewu'* family.

Over the generations, a single originative *lewu'* family might, through the processes of segmentation, give rise to a number of derivative *lewu'* families, and the latter in turn become originative *lewu'* families spawning still more derivative *lewu'* families. Technically, an originative and derivative *lewu'* family continue to share primary use rights in the same swidden plots, assuming that the absence of virgin forest in the region makes it impossible for an individual in either family to acquire any new and exclusive pioneer rights to plots in Padju Epat. However, with the passage of more time, the primary rights to some plots are gradually and informally transferred to the derivative *lewu'* family. In the early years after secession, the senior members of the derivative family would continue to farm swidden plots to which they had primary use rights mediated through the originative *lewu'* family. However, after a generation or so, the children and grandchildren in the derivative *lewu'* family would not be familiar with all of the swidden areas controlled by the originative household, but would tend to reclear the swiddens used by their parents or grandparents in the derivative family. These would have been used within their own lifetimes, and thus particular areas could be remembered. It must be stressed that this process was informal, due to the natural limitations of individual memories. As long as people in both the originative and derivative *lewu'* families were able to trace their relationship to former users of particular plots, they would be able to make use of their rights. But after the passage of two or three generations, this would become increasingly difficult to do.

Individuals who marry out of either the originative or the derivative *lewu'* family maintain only secondary or tertiary rights in the swidden plots and heirloom property of those families. Thus primary rights are maintained following segmentation, but become attenuated through exofiliation. Emigres who do not formally dissociate themselves from their Padju Epat *lewu'* families, through exofiliative marriage or segmentation, are still considered members of these groups and may at any time return to make use of the village houses and associated swidden rights; however, if the *lewu'* family house is rebuilt without their participation, emigres lose their rights in the house.

Changes in Lewu' Family Size

The size of *lewu'* families has been affected by the pattern of emigration that has become established over the last half-century in Padju Epat. Prior to World War II, the village houses of originative *lewu'* families tended to be quite large and to contain many constituent *dangau* families. Although many of the constituent *dangau* families had emigrated northward, the representatives of these families used to return once a year following harvest to participate in the *mira ka'ayat* ceremony and, coincidentally, to pay their taxes, since the Dutch colonial government counted emigres as residents of their home Padju Epat villages for tax purposes. The returned emigres assisted in the work that was necessary to keep their respective *lewu'* family houses in repair.

During World War II, the Japanese occupational government altered the region's administrative system so that emigres were taxed in the communities where they lived most of the year rather than in their villages of origin, with the result that thereafter the return of emigres to Padju Epat for *mira ka'ayat* declined each year. Under these changed circumstances, it became increasingly difficult for their few resident members to keep the large old *lewu'* family houses in repair. During the 1950's almost all of the now decrepit large houses were demolished and smaller houses built to accommodate new originative and derivative *lewu'* family configurations. The emigration of all the members of some *lewu'* families left a few houses completely deserted, and as these abandoned structures fell from dilapidation to decay, they were not replaced.

By 1964, more than half (54 percent) of Padju Epat's village houses were being used by only a single *dangau* family, while another 27 percent were occupied by two *dangau* families. Ten percent and 9 percent of the households contained respectively three and four constituent *dangau* families, and none of the village houses was being used by more than four *dangau* families.

With the effective disappearance of some *lewu'* families from Padju Epat and the decline in the size of those remaining, individual *dangau* families had more opportunity, when the need arose, to farm swidden plots to which they had only secondary, tertiary, or even residual rights, since in many cases all or most of the families holding primary rights to those plots had emigrated. Thus, those *dangau* families remaining in Padju Epat had a somewhat wider choice of swidden plots to cultivate than had been available earlier in the century.

The vesting of land rights in the bilineal *bumuh*, and the mediation of those rights through the *lewu'* family, provided a good system for keeping land resources equitably distributed throughout the community in the face of demographic fluctuations in *lewu'* family size. In a large *lewu'* family that did not control enough land to support all of its members, some members could make use of swidden plots in which they held secondary or tertiary rights, or some youthful members might be encouraged to marry into *lewu'* families whose land resources were not strained. Conversely, land controlled by small *lewu'* families that were not making full use of their resources would be available to *bumuh* members holding secondary, tertiary, or residual rights.

13

The Kindred

THE LIMITS FOR THE RECOGNITION OF KINSMEN in Padju Epat are set by the maximal *bumuh*. In Chapter 10, I indicated that in Padju Epat a *bumuh* is a kin group comprising all the descendants of a particular focal ancestor or ancestral couple. From a particular individual's point of view, those people descended from one of his pairs of great-great grandparents form a group that can be termed a maximal *bumuh*; the comembers of a maximal *bumuh* consider each other as kinsmen and accord kin terms to each other.

Ideally, the other members of a maximal *bumuh* should render assistance to a member who is sponsoring some activity such as a rice planting session or a child's naming ceremony. However, in actual practice not all members of the maximal *bumuh* render such assistance to the activity's sponsor; instead, assistance is selective and depends to a great extent on the quality of the dyadic ties linking the sponsor with each of the group's other members.

An individual may belong to as many as eight different maximal *bumuh*, that is, to as many as he has pairs of great-great grandparents. Because of the frequent occurrence of marriages between cousins, however, a person may have fewer than eight pairs of great-great grandparents and, thus, be a member of fewer than eight maximal *bumuh*.

Taking a particular individual, whom we may designate Ego, as a focus, the set of kinsmen comprising the members of all the maximal *bumuh* to which he belongs constitutes a kin category that anthropologists term a "kindred." With the exception of full siblings, no two people will have the same eight pairs of great-great grandparents and thus, will not belong to precisely the same set of maximal *bumuh*. However, there may be some overlapping of the sets of maximal *bumuh* constituting the kindreds of consanguineally related individuals. Other things being equal, first cousins will share membership in four of their respective maximal *bumuh*, second cousins in two, and third cousins in one. Although the kindreds of some people may overlap in this way, the kindreds of no two people, again excepting full siblings, are exactly the same.

A kindred is not a fixed kin group in the way that a *bumuh* is. The members of Ego's kindred may have no kin relationship to one another, unless they happen also to be members of the same maximal *bumuh*. Thus, two individuals, who are Ego's matrilateral first cousin and patrilateral first cousin respectively, are both members of Ego's kindred but may be unrelated to each other. The only person linking all the members of his kindred is the focal Ego. For this reason, anthropologists frequently refer to social categories of the kindred type as "Ego-centric" kin groups.

Although the members of Ego's kindred may have an obligation to him, they have no necessary obligations to one another unless, as pointed out earlier, they happen to be comembers of the same maximal *bumuh*. What can be described as kindred obligations stem only from common *bumuh* membership. It is for this reason that the Padju Epat kindred has no real group identity. The kindred functions as a unit only in activities sponsored by or for its focal Ego, as members of the different maximal *bumuh* to which Ego belongs fulfill their respective *bumuh* obligations to him in concert. The only other element that all members of the kindred have in common is the expectation that Ego will, in turn, participate in the kindred activities that they themselves may sponsor.

After marriage, a Padju Epat couple generally participates as a unit in fulfilling the kindred obligations of either spouse. This circumstance serves to double the effective kindred of married individuals. This enlarged kindred shared by a married couple can be termed the "extended kindred." While full siblings may share the same Ego-centric kindred, rarely will they have the same extended kindred.

Kindred Activities and Kindred Ties

The individual at the center of an Ego-centric kindred can be considered its "focal member." The activities in which people participate primarily because of a kin-based obligation to a kindred's focal member can be termed "kindred activities." Kindred activities are group activities sponsored by or for the focal member and include life-cycle ceremonies and cooperative work projects such as the clearing, planting, and harvesting of swidden fields. What one participant considers a kindred activity may be viewed as a neighborly, civic, or recreational activity by other participants. Most people engaging in a particular social activity know their reasons for doing so. At any rate, the designation of an undertaking as a "kindred activity" is related not so much to the specific nature of the activity as to the reasons for participating in it.

The relationship that exists between a focal member and a member of his kindred can be termed a "kindred tie," although it should be kept in mind that kindred ties are ultimately based on common membership in a maximal *bumuh*. A kindred tie is bidirectional. If individual A is a member of B's kindred, B is likewise a member of A's kindred.

Ideally, all the members of a kindred should participate to a certain extent in the kindred activities of its focal member. However, in practice, not all members do, so that in Padju Epat a kindred tie may be considered either active or inactive, depending on the degree of expectation there is that the individuals linked by the tie will, in fact, participate in each other's kindred activities. Where a kindred tie is active, the individuals so linked are expected to participate in each other's kindred activities, and failure to do so is given a negative assessment by the community as improper. Where a kindred tie is inactive, there is no positive expectation of participation in kindred activities, and failure to participate is assessed neutrally by the community.

An individual's kindred may be extremely large, and it would take considerable time, effort, and money for him to honor his kindred obligations toward all of them. The recognition of both active and inactive kindred ties puts practical, but flexible, limits on the extent of these obligations. This practice reduces the number of kinsmen toward whom an individual has to maintain kindred-based obligations, while at the same time maintaining the potential for establishing active kindred ties selectively, when needed, with a large and geographically dispersed group of recognized kinsmen.

From the standpoint of a kindred's focal member, it may be said that those with whom he maintains active ties constitute his "active kindred," while those with whom he has inactive ties constitute his "latent kindred." It is possible for an inactive member of a kindred to participate in an undertaking sponsored by its focal member without its being considered as kindred activity. For example, when collecting data on cooperative work groups, I found a pair of third cousins who had exchanged planting services on different days. As far as I could tell, these two normally had very little to do with each other's activities. I asked one why he had planted for the second, and was told that it was to repay a work debt, since the second had earlier planted for him. Later I asked the second man why he had planted for the first. "I went to plant for him because I heard that he was killing a pig to feed the workers. I went for the meal. Everyone was there." Both men denied that their distant kin tie had had anything to do with the situation.

Core Kindred and Kindred Pool

In Padju Epat, the members of a kindred can be divided into two groups. For the first group, active kindred membership is obligatory, and failure to participate in kindred activities is negatively assessed. This group we may call the "core kindred." The core kindred comprises the focal member, his siblings, parents, grandparents, children, grandchildren, and, if living, great grandparents and great grandchildren. If in the area and not incapacitated, the members of the core kindred should and usually do take part in kindred activities. At weddings, funerals, plantings, harvests, and any other activities sponsored by or for the focal member, the core kindred forms the nucleus of the group participating. The kindred ties linking the focal member with the members of the core kindred are active for the life of the individuals involved.

For the second group, active kindred membership is optative. This group may be termed the "kindred pool." For members of the kindred pool, the activation of kindred ties is not automatic, but left to the personal preferences of the individuals involved.

Since the kindred pool extends to third cousins in all eight maximal *bumuh*, an individual's kindred can include a large number of people. Just how many people to include is a moot point. A large number of his kindred members may be unknown to the focal member, for Padju Epaters make little attempt to memorize complete genealogies to any depth. Most people could not even name more than a few of their great grandparents, let alone the complete roster of their great-great grandparents. Where specific descent lines are remembered, they tend to be maintained in order to show an individual's links to some important ancestor. Generally speaking, the status of collateral relatives tends to be keyed to lineal relatives of the first and second ascendent generation, rather than to the more remote ancestors. Thus a person would know a second cousin more as the child of a person his father had called "first cousin" than as the great grandchild of their common ancestor. Beyond the first cousin range, it is common for two individuals to know the exact magnitude of their relationship without having the faintest idea who their common ancestor was. Even though a person may not know all of his first cousins, when he encounters one there is never any difficulty tracing the precise links that relate them. An individual will recognize many, though not all, of the siblings and first cousins of his parents and grandparents from observation or hearsay, and on this basis compute the degree of his own relationship to cousins in his own generation. Adoption and serial marriage also do their bit to obscure kindred relationships.

Establishment and Maintenance of Kindred Ties

For members of the kindred pool, common residence is an important factor in the establishment of active kindred ties. Thus all the members of the *lewu'* family are usually members of each other's active kindreds. An individual focal member whose parents settled uxorilocally may have been brought up in the same household as one or two of his mother's siblings and several matrilateral cousins. These collateral relatives will most likely have active kindred ties with the focal member, while such ties may remain inactive with the mother's nonresident siblings and some equally close patrilateral kinsmen. However, such a situation does not at all rule out the activation of kindred ties with patrilateral kinsmen; these may depend primarily on the type of relations that the focal member's parents maintain with his patrilateral relatives. Naturally, the converse situation might hold true if the focal member's parents settled virilocally.

The initial activation of kindred ties is not so much an individual concern, since they follow almost automatically from the circumstances of parental residence. However, the maintenance of these active kindred ties is a matter of personal choice. This brings us to two characteristics of active kindred ties.

The first involves the lapsing of active kindred ties, and the second, variations in kindred configurations at different stages in a focal member's life.

Active ties linking a member of a kindred to its focal member can lapse, so that the former moves into the latent kindred category. Such ties will usually be allowed to lapse at the pleasure of either member or at their mutual desire. If one member stops participating in the kindred activities of the other, the second will usually discontinue attendance at kindred activities sponsored by the first. The active ties may be severed rather suddenly, either because of an altercation or because one of the parties to the relationship has emigrated. On the other hand, the ties may gradually lapse to an inactive state because neither party cares enough to maintain the active relationship. A lapsed kindred tie may be reactivated at any time that the individuals concerned find it mutually convenient. The active ties of core kindred members never really lapse. Even if one emigrates, he will be expected to return for important kindred activities, such as marriages and funerals; if he cannot return himself, he is expected to send some monetary gift or a representative.

An individual's participation in kindred activities normally varies at different stages in his life. Children are the focus of, and participate in, a minimal amount of kindred activity. In ceremonies related to the birth or death of a child, kinsmen participate more because of kindred ties with the child's parents than because of ties with the child, though technically these latter ties exist. Since participation in kindred activities usually requires the contribution of labor, food, and money in varying proportions, a youth does not usually engage in a full range of kindred activities until after his marriage. From that time, he is on his own as far as maintaining or establishing active ties with members of his kindred pool.

Kindred ties are bidirectional, and the maintenance of an active tie indicates that each party to the relationship is participating in the other's kindred activities. Where participation involving members of the kindred pool is not bidirectional, the active kindred tie is allowed to lapse. Although active kindred ties are bidirectional, they are not always reciprocal. The distinction here between "bidirectional" and "reciprocal" needs some clarification.

Where active kindred ties link members of different generations, each must fulfill his kindred obligations to the other. However, the number and range of kindred activities in which each must participate in order to fulfill his kindred obligations are of different orders. The person of lower generation normally attends a relatively wide variety of kindred activities sponsored by the individual of higher generation, while the latter is expected to attend only the more important kindred activities sponsored for or by the former. Thus, where an active kindred tie links a man and his father's brother, the nephew will attend planting and harvesting activities and shaman ceremonies as well as the more important life-cycle ceremonies revolving around birth, marriage, and death, all sponsored by or for his uncle. In fulfilling his obligations, the uncle will generally limit his attendance to his nephew's more important kindred functions, with sporadic participation in his kindred activities of lesser consequence. In other words, the person of lower generation has to do

Raising a house frame is an activity for kindred participation.

more to keep up his end of the kindred relationship, and the disparity becomes greater as the generation differential increases. These particular kindred ties are bidirectional, to the extent that each individual is expected to
fulfill certain obligations to each other. However, the relationship is not reciprocal since their mutual obligations are of different orders. Where two individuals of the same generation are linked by kindred ties, their obligations to
each other are reciprocal in that each participates to about the same extent
in the kindred activities of the other.

Group Kindred Activities

As indicated above, the scope of expected kindred participation varies
with the importance of the activity. A very few activities, including weddings,
a few post-mortem ceremonies, and perhaps a shaman's initiation ceremony,

require the participation of the focal member's entire active kindred. A smaller attendance potential is found in various cooperative labor projects associated with the agricultural cycle or the raising of a house frame, as well as shaman curing ceremonies, children's naming ceremonies, or ritual cleansing ceremonies.

Within certain limits, the range of the kindred who participate in a particular type of activity may depend on the importance which its sponsor attaches to the activity. Padju Epaters enjoy and value an activity that is carried out with gaiety and bustle. On occasion, a focal member who is sponsoring an ordinarily minor kindred activity may decide to make it into a really big affair. If the project is a house-raising, which can ordinarily be accomplished by eight or ten people, only some of whom are participating on a kindred basis, the sponsor will announce his intention to kill a pig or two, making a celebration out of the affair. Many people will attend, and with them a large segment of the active kindred. Of course, kindred members rarely need urging to attend such a gay affair. Nonetheless, light as the burden may be, they still have an obligation to attend. In general, the greater the value that the sponsor puts on a given activity, as evidenced by his announcements and preparations, the greater the obligation of the active kindred to attend. If a member of the general community does not attend such an affair, it is merely remarked that "Pa' Djudi missed a pretty good party." But if a member of the active kindred is absent without apparent reason, tongues will wag as to the future course of relations between the host and the absentee. Such an occurrence could signal the incipient lapsing of an active kindred tie.

Participation in a kindred activity, however, does not necessarily entail the actual physical presence of kindred members. A participant usually donates food, labor, and money in varying combinations or amounts, in accordance with the proximity of the kindred relationship and the relative importance of the activity. Although personal attendance is desirable at certain kindred functions, the donation of food and/or money will suffice to fulfill the kindred obligation.

Dyadic Kindred Activities

It should be apparent that a kindred tie is basically a dyadic relationship involving pairs of kinsmen. With the exception of those involving members of the core kindred, these ties are activated and maintained on a voluntary basis. The activation of a kindred tie indicates the willingness of the two individuals involved in the relationship to assist each other in various activities. So far I have limited my discussion to a set of rather formalized, recurrent, and mostly ceremonial activities in which a number of people participate because each has an active kindred tie with the same single individual.

Equally important, however, are the activities in which two or three individuals linked by kindred ties may participate on a less formal basis; these may involve the making of a canoe, a joint fishing expedition, a rattan cutting project, or some other undertaking of mutual interest. Such activities are arranged on a piecemeal basis, and may or may not include other people. By their very nature, participation is not required. If a man wants to build a large canoe and has found a likely tree, he may approach a kindred member known to be an expert boatbuilder to suggest a joint venture, in which the profits from the canoe's sale would be split. The boatbuilder may accept the proposal or not, depending upon his own inclination. Where there are several expert canoebuilders in the village, it is natural first to approach one with whom an active kindred tie is maintained, for an outsider would demand a higher percentage of the profits. Similarly, where a person contracts to tap another's rubber trees, the tapper will receive a larger percentage of the profits if he has an active kindred tie with the owner than if no such tie existed.

The exercising of individual kindred ties in such an informal manner is as important to the dynamics of kindred relationships as participation in more formal activities which involve the kindred as a group. The two forms of activity, dyadic and group, are complementary elements in the structure of kindred relationships. The individual who does not fulfill his obligations in kindred group activities will receive no special consideration in dyadic activities. Where an active kindred relationship exists in dyadic activities, participation in Ego-based group activities is expected.

The Activation of Kindred Ties

Heretofore the activation of kindred ties has been described in static terms: that is, ties have been considered either active or inactive. The activation of kindred ties can in fact also be seen as a process through which a formerly latent relationship passes to an active state. The potential for kindred tie activation is an important feature not only of the kindred system itself but of the larger Padju Epat social structure as well.

The kindred system contains a built-in mechanism for the activation of its ties. An individual owes a certain generalized obligation to members of his latent kindred. If a member of the latent kindred comes to its focal member and specifically invokes his kindred tie in asking some service, it cannot be honorably denied without good reason. The utilization of this mechanism is not too important in an individual's home area, where the basis for active kindred ties may be built up gradually from childhood, but it takes on real significance when a person lives or travels outside his home district. If he visits an emigre settlement, for instance, he will look up any kinsmen he knows to be resident there. If he has no known kindred in the area, he will seek out emigres from his home village and often find among them some with whom he has unsuspected latent kindred ties. Where kindred ties are found, hospitality is automatically extended to the stranger. If he gets along well with the host family and decides to settle down in the emigre village, the relationship will be maintained as an active kindred tie. On the other hand, if he does not hit it off very well with the host family, he will probably move out as soon as possible, and no attempt will be made by either party to establish an active kindred tie. Such limited obligation toward latent kindred provides the opportunity for the establishment of an active kindred relationship on a trial basis. If the relationship proves satisfactory, mutual participation in dyadic and group kindred activities will be regularized. If the relationship is unsatisfactory, it continues as a latent tie. Because of the wide distribution of Padju Epat emigre families, an individual can find members of his kindred in many areas, and the knowledge that he has kindred in certain settlements often dictates his itinerary when making a trip.

Affinal Kinsmen and Kindred Membership

In terms of effective kin ties, the kindreds of both spouses become merged after marriage to form what I have already termed the extended kindred. Since participation in a kindred group activity often requires a contribution of food or money, such an undertaking involves the whole *dangau* family and not just individuals. A contribution of rice made to a kindred activity comes from the *dangau* family supply, while the same holds true for cash donations. It is the *dangau* family as a unit that participates, and the kindred obligations of both spouses are honored by the family. If a man attends a house-raising sponsored by his uncle, his wife will usually help with the food preparation and cooking. At one funeral ceremony in Siong, one man who attended came down from an emigre village because the deceased was his wife's grandmother; his wife remained at home because she had recently had a child, and Padju Epat *adat* does not allow a new mother to attend death ceremonies. The *adat* head of Murutuwu felt obliged to attend the same funeral because, as he said, "The dead woman was my wife's aunt." Actually, the deceased was his wife's mother's brother's wife. Thus it would appear that in terms of practical considerations, a person counts his spouse's active kindred as his own.

14

The Life Cycle

Birth

A PADJU EPATER FIRST SEES THE LIGHT OF DAY in the presence of a small audience. The baby's mother is attended by her mother or mother-in-law (depending on locus of residence), a midwife, and her husband. If the birth takes place in the village, then the women of the *lewu'* family and neighboring households will offer help taking care of older children or assisting with household chores. The midwife is usually an elderly woman with long experience in delivering babies, but occasionally an old man may serve in this role. The old *adat* head of Telang had been that village's most skilled midwife until his eyesight failed. The government maintains a school in Bandjarmasin for training midwives in modern techniques, but the nearest graduate of this institution is located in Tamiang Layang, too far away to be of any service to Padju Epat.

Childbirth is an extremely traumatic experience for a Padju Epat woman, since she always knows that, if problems arise in the delivery, long hours of pain and perhaps death await her. To minimize her difficulties, propitiatory ceremonies are given in the final weeks of pregnancy, and some families promise an offering to an ancestral spirit if the birth is accomplished without complications. A successful delivery is greeted with much relief by the whole family.

Following birth, the house in which the baby was born becomes ritually unclean, and its members are put in a state of ritual danger. If the birth has taken place in the village house, all resident members of the *lewu'* family are affected. During the period of ritual pollution no ceremonies can be performed in the affected house, nor should members of the family participate in outside ceremonies. Thus many women choose to have babies in swidden huts in order not to encumber the entire *lewu'* family with the ritual pollution accompanying birth.

After successful childbirth, a new mother does not find much immediate relief. For a period of one to two weeks she is not allowed to leave the house, is supposed to sit up rather than recline, and is allowed to eat nothing but rice, although with the spread of modern health education, many of these traditional practices are no longer observed. When the baby's umbilical stump falls off eight to fifteen days after birth, a naming ceremony is held in the village house. During the ceremony a shaman performs a cleansing ritual that purifies the house and its occupants, the midwife is honored and given presents by the baby's family, and the baby is given a personal name. Relatives and other villagers are invited to the ceremony to feast and meet the new baby. After the completion of the naming ceremony, the mother is released from her dietary and other post-partum restrictions, and the household returns to a normal ritual state.

The mother resumes her duties within the *dangau* family as soon as she is able, and is quickly doing heavy work again. The mother carries the baby with her, tied close to her side in a sling, as she goes about her work, and breastfeeds it on demand. However, the baby may be left in the village occasionally if there is another lactating woman in the *lewu'* family who will nurse the child. By the age of three months, the baby is offered some solid food in the form of mashed bananas, but will continue to be nursed to a certain extent until another baby comes along to command the mother's attention. In such cases, weaning is abrupt, and the child must learn to adjust to his new position in life outside the immediate focus of his mother's attention. If no younger sibling follows, weaning is a very casual process, and a child may continue to nurse until it is four or five years old, although an occasional child of seven may still find sporadic solace at his mother's breast.

Life for a Padju Epat baby is highly gratifying. Whenever it cries it is immediately offered a breast, that of its mother or of some other woman in the household. It is constantly fondled and made much of by a myriad of indulgent relatives. The sounds of a baby's cries bring anguish to the heart of a Padju Epater, and immediate steps are always taken to pacify an unhappy baby. When the infant is not being carried around by its mother, it is bundled snugly and immovably into a sling, made of a bolt of cloth, that is suspended from the rafters of the house, in which it is gently swung back and forth by a member of the household, often a two- or three-year-old sibling. Passivity is encouraged in the young child. When riding at its mother's hip or in its pendulous swing the infant's movements are extremely restricted. When it gets old enough to sit up by itself, the baby's activities are still constrained. Since crawling is considered a type of behavior more suitable for animals than people, babies are picked up if they try to crawl; babies who cannot yet walk are carried most of the time, usually by somewhat older siblings. With this kind of training, babies soon learn to stay still, and it is not unusual to see one sitting quietly for long periods of time. Only when a child has learned to walk at about the age of a year is it allowed to move around from place to place under its own power. Little attempt is made at toilet training. Young infants defecate and urinate wherever they happen to be. If an adult manages to catch a baby in time, it will be held over the edge of the front porch or floor slats in the kitchen so that the excreta does not soil the house floor. After children are old enough to walk, they are clothed in an upper garment only, boys in a shirt and girls in a dress, and encouraged to play outside the house. As children get older, their parents will attempt to inculcate them in the proprieties of bodily elimination by the use of cajolery and finally mockery. Eventually, and in their own good time, children toilet train themselves. When I was collecting information on Padju Epat's recent history, men frequently informed me in a fondly joking manner that such and such an event happened, "Before I wore pants."

Childhood

Once they are able to toddle around, children spend much of their time playing around the village, nominally in the care of an elder sibling or cousin. Gradually they are given a few light responsibilities commensurate with their abilities. A two-year-old child may be left in the village to tend a baby sibling, by pushing it gently back and forth in its rafter sling. A three- or four-year-old may frequently be seen struggling about the village with a baby on its hip, while trying to keep up with the play activities of its peer group. Slightly older children will be asked to help in lighter household chores such as gathering firewood, carrying water, and husking rice.

Life is not completely carefree for the Padju Epat child, however. From the time of birth on, he is attacked by various diseases, infections, and parasites. Malaria and dysentery, which are endemic in the region, take a heavy toll among young children. Pneumonia, respiratory infections, intestinal worms, and infected cuts all afflict young children, weakening and often killing them. About one third of all children born do not survive to adulthood.

By the age of six or seven, children begin to provide useful assistance to their families in agricultural work. They help with planting, weeding, the guarding of crops, and other tasks that are not too strenuous, although considerable time is still devoted to play. Boys perform tasks appropriate to men, and little girls help their mothers. Play groups, earlier composed of both sexes, now normally consist of either boys or girls.

At seven, most children begin their primary education in one of Padju Epat's elementary schools. Families differ in the importance that is attached to formal education. Today, most children stay in school for five or six years, although school is generally recessed during the peak work periods of the agricultural calendar. As children get older, and become capable of increasingly useful subsistence work, the school attendance of some becomes more and more sporadic as they assume a greater share of their family's work burden. This may be true particularly in the case of an eldest child, especially a girl. On the other hand, some families place a high premium on education and will encourage their children to stay in school as long as possible, often at great sacrifice to the parents.

Older children of ten to fourteen are expected to perform regular agricultural and household tasks as they learn the roles assigned to their sex. At this stage of life, a child may spend many hours assisting an elderly grandparent, probably receiving more indulgent treatment from the latter than from his own parents. Often a child will begin to study to become a shaman, or learn traditional lore from his close association with an old man who is an *adat* law expert.

Adolescence and Courtship

From the age of about fourteen on through adolescence, young people's thoughts are turned to courtship and marriage. In Padju Epat, sexual relations are believed a ritually dangerous activity which may be entered into only by individuals who have received the proper ritual protection that is vested in a couple as a part of the marriage ceremony. Indulgence in illicit sexual relations places not only the participants but the community at large in a dangerous state of ritual imbalance. Nonetheless, a certain amount of premarital sexual activity does take place in Padju Epat, but such behavior is minimal in comparison with that described in a number of other Dayak groups.

Padju Epat society does, however, provide institutionalized opportunities for young people of opposite sexes to mingle and flirt. At planting parties during the agricultural season, many of the unmarried youths foresake their male role of dibbling to join the ladies, where they cluster like bees around the prettiest young girls. During rest breaks in other cooperative activities, too, the young men and women have a chance to eye each other, tell riddles, and giggle incessantly. Whenever a village household puts on a large ceremony, such as a wedding or shaman curing ritual, a small coterie of young people always hangs about the front porches, engaged in halting but animated conversation. There is no doubt that some young people are in potential ritual danger at such times.

Opportunities for supervised flirting are also provided by occasional village-sponsored dancing parties. Although a variety of traditional and pseudo-traditional dances are performed at these parties, the most popular dance among the young of both sexes is *giring-giring*, representing a stylized mock combat in which the performers, who dance in pairs, compete against one another. In their competition, each "antagonist" maintains a fixed beat with a rattle held in one hand, while beating out complex syncopations on the ground with a stick held in the other. He attempts to confuse his partner and, thus, cause him to falter in the dance. While the rattling and pounding is going on, each dancer also tries to work out a series of complicated dance steps and leaps without falling victim to his "opponent's" rhythmic blandishments. Such dancing sessions might last all night. There is no set time of year for this type of dancing to be held, and indeed, as with our own teenagers, it seems to run in fads. There may be no dances for months at a time, and then one village will hold a session, after which it catches on like wildfire for a month or two

A young girl helping her mother husk rice for their dangau *family.*

of weekly or even nightly outings, after which the dancing fades from the scene.

On market days, and at the time of the big ceremonial occasions such as *idjambe*, the village cafes serve as congregating spots for young people of both sexes, much as our soda fountains and drive-in dairy bars do. It is under such relatively controlled, public conditions that young people get the chance to mix with members of the opposite sex.

Young men approaching marriageable age (around eighteen or twenty) frequently leave Padju Epat, visit relatives in emigre villages, and look over the crop of girls. Often an acquaintanceship established in this way will lead fairly quickly to marriage by elopement. But sexual experimentation is not a normal part of the Padju Epat premarital experience. No matter how much the young men would like to shop around, the girls of marriageable age (fifteen to eighteen) are generally looking for husbands and not experimental paramours. If a couple has developed an attachment and plans to marry, they may, if they have the opportunity, sleep together a few times before going through the formality of eloping, or getting their parents to arrange a marriage. Anything more experimental is considered extremely risky business both ritually and socially.

Marriage

In Padju Epat, marriages may be initiated in two ways: by parental arrangement or by elopement. Arranged marriage has been the traditional form, but elopement is now more common. Of the 258 marriages, both extant and past, ever entered into by the current residents of Telang, Siong, and Murutuwu, 55 percent had been arranged and 45 percent were by elopement.

If a boy and girl agree that they want to get married, they may elope. Lest there be any confusion, the term "elopement" should not be interpreted to mean that the couple runs off to get married. The act of "eloping" is merely a first step in initiating marriage proceedings.

When a couple decides to elope, they go together to the house of the village *adat* head or that of a responsible mutual friend. There they announce that they wish to be married. Then the *adat* head or the friend goes to inform the family representatives of both the boy and girl. If either is from another village, usually a brother, uncle, or other relative in the village can act as his representative; if not, the proceedings may be delayed a day or two until a member of the more immediate family arrives from his home village.

The family representatives and any available village elders gather to discuss the matter. If there are no objections to the proposed marriage, a contract is negotiated, and a provisional wedding performed, a ceremony termed "half-marriage." Thereafter, the couple are ritually and legally sanctioned to live together for a period of three months, during which time they must raise the money to finance a regular marriage ceremony. If the couple hopes to acquire the amount of money necessary for the complete marriage ceremony, they need some help from their respective families. Frequently they will be allowed to spend all their time tapping family-owned rubber trees, and permitted to keep all the proceeds.

Not all elopements lead to a half-marriage. If one or both of the family spokesmen are against the marriage for any reason, the whole affair may be terminated then and there, without the half-marriage being performed. Objections may range from generalized disapproval of the marriage, to a failure to reach accord on a particular article of the marriage agreement, such as marriage payments or residence. During the half-marriage period, the couple usually lives with the family with whom they expect to take up residence after the full marriage. This gives everybody a chance to get adjusted to one another.

If at the end of the half-marriage period one or the other spouse does not want to go through with the full marriage, formal divorce proceedings must be instituted and the case heard by the adjudicating elders. The person at fault is made to pay damages, and if the girl is pregnant, the man must pay a rather large compensatory fine. One of the important sections of the marriage agreement contracted at the time of the half-marriage ceremony deals with the nature of the contingent penalties to be assessed in the event that the union is terminated before the full marriage has taken place.

In the more traditional arranged marriage, negotiations are handled entirely by the families of the prospective bride and groom. Marriage arrangements are sometimes entered into at the instigation of the boy and girl themselves, but often are begun without their even having been consulted. An occasional marriage will be arranged against the opposition of the boy or girl.

Marriage arrangements are initiated by the head of the boy's *lewu'* family, who acts as his representative. He approaches the girl's family informally to ask if she is already betrothed and, if not, if they are willing to consider a marriage with the boy of his family. If they are, the boy's representative gives a length of cloth to the girl's family, which, when accepted, signifies that formal negotiations may begin. At this point, each *lewu'* family will notify its absent members to apprise them of the situation, solicit their opinions, and request their presence at the formal betrothal ceremony. A date is set for the betrothal ceremony, and in the interim representatives of the two families meet to work out the actual details of the marriage contract which will be announced at that time.

The formal betrothal ceremony is a big affair. Representatives of all the constituent *dangau* families in the *lewu'* families of the prospective bride and groom should attend if possible, as should the active members of their respective kindreds. The village *adat* head should be present, and, if the wedding is an important one, the custodians of the involved *tambak* groups as well. The betrothal session is fairly protracted, since the real business cannot begin until each notable has made a humorous speech. The guests settle down to enjoy an hour or two of verbal entertainment, for the ceremonial speeches, which are considered Padju Epat's premier art form, will be delivered by highly skilled practitioners of the art. The opening speech is made by the *adat* head. Then in turn the various family heads, first on the groom's, and then on the bride's, sides deliver short speeches, all in pretty much the same vein. Each speaker expresses complete astonishment at the presence of so many people in the house and cannot imagine the reason for the convocation. Each relates how he had planned to be elsewhere that evening and then recounts a humorous series of fictitious events that brought him, purely by chance, to this house full of people. Each concludes by asking that somebody, please, tell him why everyone is here. Finally the spokesman for the prospective groom arises, to say that he had not expected so much fuss, and that he had only dropped by to discuss a relatively unimportant matter. Someone in the groom's coterie pushes forward a package, and after staring at it for a while in seeming bewilderment, the groom's spokesman agrees to open it for the inspection of anyone who might be interested. The package turns out to contain gifts for the bride: these should always consist of a length of fine batik cloth and usually good material for a blouse as well. The package will also contain some money, the amount depending on the status and affluence of the families concerned. The gifts are handed over to the bride's representative, and the ceremony continues with the reading or recitation of the terms of the marriage contract, which had been agreed to prior to the betrothal ceremony. The contract sets a place and date for the wedding, specifying the penalty to be assessed against the party at fault should the agreement be broken. The contract stipulates the payments to be made, usually by the family of the groom to that of the bride, and the amount of bride service, if any, required of the groom. It should establish the locus of post-marital residence and *lewu'* family affiliation. Finally, responsibility for paying the wedding costs is assigned.

Neither bride nor groom is supposed to witness the ceremony, but usually the girl eavesdrops in an inner room, while the boy makes himself inconspicuous on the front porch. When the terms of the contract have been made public, the bride and groom, bashful and giggling, are allowed to show themselves. Small amounts of money are distributed to the village *adat* head, to any elders present, and to many of the guests. Traditionally, the terms of the marriage contract were memorized by the representatives of each prospective spouse and also by a number of the witnesses, and it was for this service that "witness" money was distributed. Nowadays, many marriage contracts are written, at least in abbreviated form, and signed by the principals, their representatives, and the *adat* head. Finally, a festive meal is served to everybody. In a Christian ceremony, the guests depart after the meal, but in an animist affair, rice beer will be brought out to celebrate the occasion.

After the betrothal ceremony, the couple returns to their respective homes to await the appointed nuptial day. They may not live together until after the actual wedding has been performed, and in this respect, an arranged marriage differs greatly from the initial half-marriage ceremony performed in the case of an elopement.

Marriage ceremonies are even gayer affairs than betrothals. Family and kindred members from distant villages return to the households of bride and groom the day before the ceremony. Food is prepared at the bride's house, and a pig slaughtered for the wedding meal. Amid great merriment and joking, the groom and his party walk to the bride's house. The groom is led to a seat next to the bride, atop a pile of huge bronze gongs decorated with leaves and surrounded with offerings to placate the spirits. Speeches are made as the assembled guests contribute small amounts of money to the couple. As before, the speeches are humorous, and a well-turned phrase heightens the hilarity of the crowd. In the final speech a senior family member instructs the new couple on married life. The ritual for the actual marriage is performed first by the *adat* head, who takes a frond of leaves, dips them in the blood of the sacrificed pig, and sprinkles the couple lightly. Then other elders are invited to sanctify the marriage bond in the same way. Often it seemed that the more distant the elder's village, the more efficacious his blessing of the new marriage, for I was always invited to participate in this part of the ritual. Once the blessing with blood has been accomplished, the couple are finally allowed to leave their uncomfortable perch on the gongs, and a meal is served to everyone. Rice beer is brought out after the meal, whereupon the elders or any accomplished musicians sing long epics of bygone days.

In the negotiations associated with both elopement and arranged marriages, one of the most important issues to be settled by the families involved is the matter of post-marital *lewu'* family affiliation, for the couple will derive its primary land-use rights and *tambak* group membership from the *lewu'* family that it joins. Although Padju Epat's basic *adat* legal regulation covering post-marital residence stipulates that the husband will "follow" his wife and join her natal *lewu'* family, in its practical flexibility, the *adat* code also enumerates a schedule of fines, the payment of which will permit the couple to join the husband's *lewu'* family, either immediately after the marriage, or after a period of "bride service" ranging from two to five years. The *adat* code may be flexibly interpreted so that a specific marriage agreement can alter the amounts to be paid or specify an intermediate length of bride service, such as one, three, or four years. As it turns out, in about half of all Padju Epat marriages, the couple ultimately affiliates with the husband's *lewu'* family.

Frequently, the couple is absorbed temporarily into the natal *dangau* family of the endofiliative spouse immediately after marriage, forming a complete stem family. This provides the couple with a modicum of guidance in the early years of their married life, but puts a certain strain on an exofiliative spouse, who must adapt himself to a dependent's role in a strange *dangau* family. If bride service is to be performed, the newly married couple is always absorbed into the wife's natal *dangau* family in this way, and remains a part of it until the period of bride service is completed. In this latter case, according to *adat*, when the period of bride service is finished, the departing couple has no right to take anything with them from the bride's house. However, this provision is more honored in the breach than in the observance. If the relationship between the departing couple and the wife's parents is a warm one, they are usually allowed to take any property, except rice, that they have acquired during the period of bride service. On the other hand, when relations are not good, the couple might depart empty-handed. One older man told me that he and his wife left her house with only the clothes on their backs, so great had been the animosity between them and her parents. Potential tensions between an individual and his in-laws can be lessened when a marriage between cousins occurs (about 30 percent of the 258 marriages on which I collected data were of this type), for then the inmarrying spouse already has an established kin relationship with his in-laws.

The Establishment of an Independent Family

When a child is born, the new couple finally become adults in the eyes of the community. The teknonyms acquired as parents symbolize the passage of the boy and girl from the status of dependent children into that of responsible adults. With the birth of their first child, the couple has taken the initial step toward the establishment of their own independent *dangau* family.

After a few years of marriage, or with the completion of bride service, the couple will secede from the parental *dangau* family to establish an independent nuclear *dangau* family of its own, with *lewu'* family affiliation following the marriage agreement. The couple's independent status receives symbolic recognition when their own rice strain is created from a mixture of the rice strains of each spouse's natal *dangau* family in a rice seed "wedding" ritual.

With independence, the couple settles into the routine life of the Padju Epater. They rise with the dawn, bathe and wash clothes in the river, and breakfast on cold leftover rice, a little fruit, and maybe some coffee, before commencing the day's business. In the late morning the women prepare the day's main meal, consisting of hot rice, a soup made of vegetables with perhaps a little fresh meat or fish, some dried fish, hot chili peppers, fruit in season, and well sweetened tea or coffee. The family returns to its afternoon's work, which is broken midway for a snack consisting of fried bananas or pieces of cassava boiled or fried and dipped in sugar. Another bath and clotheswashing session follows the completion of the day's work. A light supper is usually a warmed-over version of the lunch menu. In the evening, the family sits gossiping by the light of a candle or small kerosene lantern, planning the following day's activities while the women mend clothes or plait baskets, and the men smoke and relax. By nine o'clock or so, the family is asleep, leaving a small light to break the darkness and give comfort to the restive.

Of course, a considerable amount of variety is woven into this basic routine. During some parts of the year, the family makes much use of its village house, where the presence of other *dangau* families adds a certain bustle and conviviality to the scene. Meals are more festive. One or two babies may be swinging lightly to and fro in their hanging slings, tended by a grandmother or elder sibling. Children rush in and out of the house, wheedling snacks, and scamper about the village, playing games, climbing trees, swimming in the river, and getting into all sorts of mischief. In the early morning and late afternoon, groups of women gather at the river's edge, bathing, washing clothes, and gossiping. In the evening, there is frequent visiting from one household to another, and the sounds of a small gong orchestra can often be heard emanating from one or another of the houses.

By contrast, life in the swidden hut is much quieter, although a family whose *dangau* is located in a hamlet may find the pace of social life somewhat livelier than that of one occupying a relatively isolated farmstead.

Weekly attendance at the market offers a change from the normal daily routine. On Monday afternoon and evening, itinerant tradesmen begin to arrive in Telang by bicycle or boat, and the town's cafes do a thriving trade late into the night. The young men strike up a soccer game in an upper field. On Tuesday mornings, people stream into the market area, bringing a variety of vegetables, fruit, fish, rubber, and other items for sale. People gossip while buying and selling, or sit in the crowded cafes, sipping coffee, munching snacks, and watching the market activity. Some of the men while away their time and money gambling, more or less discreetly, in one of the houses located away from the main market area. Christian families have an additional opportunity for socializing at the Wednesday evening prayer meetings and the Sunday morning church services in their village.

The family can also look forward to some variety in its diet. Various forest fruits, in season, supplement cultivated pineapples and bananas. Eggs laid by its chickens appear sporadically and in unpredictable places. Fresh fish, forest birds, and fruit bats are available at some periods of the year, and a family can anticipate the occasional lucky day when one of its spear traps catches a deer or wild pig. And a family can expect to taste the meat of domestic animals, slaughtered and served at ceremonies or agricultural cooperative work sessions which they sponsor themselves or attend.

Although it must respond to the general requirements of the agricultural cycle, there is considerable flexibility in the family's daily work activities. Fishing, hunting, rubber tapping, housebuilding and repair, canoemaking, fruit gathering, and agricultural work bring variety to a demanding and unending work schedule which, even during moments of comparative rest, keeps people busy making or repairing tools, cutting rattan strips, weaving mats or baskets, and mending clothes.

Periodic crises may interrupt the family routine. The birth or marriage of a child, an accident or sickness in the family, a poor harvest, a squabble with other members of the *lewu'* family may upset the normal course of family life. Occasionally, enmity may develop between spouses, bringing disharmony to the *dangau* family itself. If the breach is too great to be bridged, a divorce may result. Divorce is fairly easy to obtain in Padju Epat, and although it is not considered a good thing *per se*, it is thought to be the logical course when spouses are truly incompatible. In Padju Epat, about 17 percent of the people who had ever been married have been involved in at least one divorce. Divorce proceedings are heard by the adjudicating elders, who attempt to ascertain which spouse, if either, is at fault. A person found to be at fault must pay damages to the other spouse. Often the amount of damages to be paid in the event of a divorce has been stipulated in the agreement contracted at the time of the marriage negotiations. After a divorce, the exofiliative spouse generally becomes reaffiliated with his or her natal family. Younger children usually stay with their mother, but the actual disposition, especially of older children, is worked out by the adjudicating elders in accordance with principles of equity and the desires of the children themselves.

Infrequently, a husband may decide to make life more interesting by taking a second wife, a step that is allowed by the Padju Epat *adat* code. Any man may take a second wife, given she is willing, by making a marriage payment to her family. Theoretically, a man who takes a second wife may either set up a separate household for her, or bring her into the menage with his first wife. In the latter case, he should have the first wife's permission and, according to *adat* law, should pay her a cash compensation. In most cases where it is tried, the single household arrangement does not work out very well; either the new wife must be put in separate quarters, or one of the wives is divorced. Polygyny, though allowed, is not highly regarded in the Padju Epat community at large, and only about 4 percent of all marriages are of this sort.

Of course, divorce and polygyny do not affect the vast majority of Padju Epat families, but the passing years do bring changes to them and their focal couples. The widowed mother of one of the spouses may join the *dangau* family to live out her final years, or the orphaned child of a sibling may be adopted into the family. Children grow up, marry, and secede to form their own *dangau* families. Perhaps one or two children will pass their high school entrance examinations and move to some distant administrative center, first to continue their education and then to take up government posts as teachers or minor officials. Their official positions seldom allow such children to return to their natal villages except for short visits. Over the years, a couple may see the other constituent families of their *lewu'* family emigrate to the north where agricultural conditions are better; many families may farm in the north for ten or fifteen years and then return to their home village, while others emigrate for life, coming back to Padju Epat only occasionally to feed their ancestral spirits and cremate their dead.

Old Age and Death

With advancing age, a couple begins to farm swiddens that lie relatively close to the village, so that they will not have to do too much walking back and forth. They are assisted in their work by grandchildren or great grandchildren, some of whom may temporarily join their *dangau* family.

Aging Padju Epaters are sensitive to the approach of death and often take steps to meet it. An old man may go into the forest, select a likely tree, fell it, and from it hew a rough boat-shaped coffin for himself or his wife. He will not put the finishing touches on the coffin, for that work should be completed by his kindred members when they attend his funeral. The coffin is simply leaned up against the side of his field hut, where it remains, perhaps for years, ready for use. Occasionally, an old person will simply decide that it is time to die, and do so. One elderly Siong lady, who though failing still appeared pretty strong, calmly announced one day that she would be gone within a week; seven days later she died.

When death does come to a Padju Epater, it is signaled to the community at large by the wailing of women and the thundering boom of great bronze gongs. As the dolorous message of the gongs is carried to the countryside, people return from their swiddens to see who has died and, if kindred obligations require it, to assist in the funeral preparations. Runners are sent to notify close relatives of the deceased who are too far away to hear the gongs.

Throughout the day of the death and the following night, close relatives gather at the bereaved home. The corpse is washed, dressed in fine clothes, and laid out in the main room of the house beneath a covering of gorgeously decorated cloth. Other bolts of cloth are hung from the walls and ceiling, and stacks of bronze gongs, pedestaled trays, and ceramic plates, culled from heirloom hoards of the *lewu'* family and related *bumuh*, are placed around the corpse. Incense sticks are burned to cover the rising smell emanating from the corpse, which ripens rapidly in the warm, humid atmosphere. If a rough coffin has not already been prepared in advance, several close male kinsmen go to the forest to make one. During the night, women of the kindred not actively engaged in wailing busy themselves preparing food for the morrow's guests.

On the day following the death, the funeral ceremony is held. Kinsmen and friends of the deceased arrive from near and far to view the corpse and attend the obsequy. The guests sit in the house or on the porch, observing the ongoing activities, talking around the intermittent sounds of gongs and wailing, perhaps discussing some of the finer pieces of heirloom property on display. Men put the finishing touches on the coffin behind the house. When the coffin is prepared, it is brought into the house and put down next to the corpse. Bits of hair and fingernails are clipped from the body by close family members, and then, amidst a rising crescendo of wails and the sounding of gongs, the corpse is lifted and wedged into the none-too-roomy coffin. As swiftly as possible, so as to stifle the odors rising from the disturbed body, the lid is placed on the coffin, sealed with resin and bound with rattan cords. A long carrying pole is then lashed lengthwise to the top of the coffin.

If the deceased died by violence, accident, or in childbirth, the corpse is ritually unclean and must be purified. The assembled adjudicating elders discuss and then rectify any ritual difficulties associated with the corpse. Then, the closest relative of the dead person gives a funeral oration, recounting the high points in the life of the departed person, and enumerating all of his progeny. At the completion of the oration, two young men, relatives of the deceased, raise the carrying pole to their shoulders and, amidst a final furious burst of gongs, rush the coffin out of the house, down the front steps, and along the village street toward the cemetery. The carriers of the aromatic coffin are changed frequently as the funeral procession passes through the village at a dog trot. Amidst a final outburst of wailing, the coffin is lowered into a prepared grave and covered with earth. Over the grave is built a small structure within which are placed the clothes and bedding of the deceased, and on the outside ritual food offerings are placed to sustain the departed spirit. When everything is completed at the cemetery, all the guests return to the village for a meal at the house of the deceased.

The attentions of the living to the dead do not end with the funeral. The spirit of the dead person must be fed periodically until his remains have been cremated. Seven days after the funeral, a small ceremony is held in which food is taken to the grave and a meal is served to attending kindred members. Forty-nine days after the funeral, another ceremony is held which is often a big affair lasting for two days and attended by a large crowd of kinsmen and others. A pig is killed, and rice beer is often brewed for this ceremony. On the second day, traditional speeches are made amidst feasting and fairly heavy imbibing. Those who can still stand, often just the women, then carry food and a little drink to the grave. Following harvest each year between the funeral and cremation, the spirit of the dead person must be fed in a small ceremony. One of the attractions of Christianity is that Christian families do not give the often expensive post-funerary ceremonies that drain the resources of animist families.

After some years, when the village cemetery begins to get crowded, the village elders will decide that it is time to hold a cremation ceremony. A date is set for the beginning of the ceremony, and the costs assessed to participants are decided upon. Messages are sent to all of the emigre settlements informing resident Padju Epaters of the arrangements. Each person to be cremated has a sponsor, a close kinsman who is responsible for paying a share of the ceremony's costs and for assisting in the accomplishment of the many work projects that must be completed before and during the ceremony.

A month or so before the start of the ceremony, the work of repairing the village ceremonial hall begins. Then a day or two before the cremation is to get underway, emigres begin to appear in the village, carrying the exhumed remains of a corpse in a basket or other receptacle. Refreshment stalls spring up along the village street to provide food for the large number of people, participants and others, who will throng into the village.

The cremation ceremony runs continuously for nine days and nights. On each day special work must be performed: the men must build or repair various parts of the ceremonial hall or cremation structure; the women fashion numerous ritual ornaments for use in the ceremony. One group of special female shamans prepares food for the spirits of the dead, while another chants incantations directing the spirits along the difficult path to the afterworld. Each day, every participating *tambak* group must slaughter a pig and provide roosters to represent them in sessions of ritual cockfighting. At the ceremonial hall the shamans continue their incantations throughout the night, and each evening the elders consume rice beer and make speeches until the early hours of the morning. On the eighth day a water buffalo is slaughtered. At frequent intervals, food is provided at the ceremonial hall for participants and spectators.

In the course of the ceremony the bones of the dead are exhumed from the village graveyard and cleaned. Special coffins are made, and into each are placed the remains of ten or twelve individuals belonging to the same *tambak* group. The coffins are then carried into the ceremonial hall, where they lie stacked on a boat-like structure throughout most of the ceremony. On the last day of the ceremony, the coffins are carried out of the ceremonial hall to the cremation structure in the forest. One or two at a time, the coffins are placed on the cremation platform and ignited, nowadays with the help of a little kerosene. If two coffins are burned simultaneously, they must represent the same *tambak* group. As a coffin is being consumed by the fire, it bursts open, spilling ashes and charred bones out onto the burning platform. When these remains have cooled, they are raked up, placed in a bronze gong, and sprinkled with coconut milk to purify them. When all the coffins have been burned, the ash-laden gongs are carried to their respective *tambak* and their contents placed inside. After covering and surrounding the various *tambak* with clothes, plates, baskets, and other items which have been ritually ripped or broken, the participants and spectators troop back to the ceremonial hall for one last meal, after which a senior *adat* specialist recapitulates the meaning of the ceremony and enumerates any errors that may have been committed in its performance.

By the end of the ninth day, all the participants in the ceremony are mentally, physically, and, perhaps, economically exhausted. In the cathartic relief that follows the completion of the ceremony, the living can accept with equanimity that the ties binding them to their dead relatives are irrevocably severed—unless one should chance to return as a *nanyu'*.

Glossary

Adat: Custom, tradition, or more narrowly, customary law.

Adat HEAD: The senior *adat* adjudicating elder of a village.

AFFINAL KINSMEN OR RELATIVES: An individual's kinsmen by marriage, *i.e.,* his in-laws. This class includes such categories as husband, wife, sibling-in-law, parent-in-law, and child-in-law.

BALAWA: One of the Padju Epat villages.

BANDJAR: A coastal Malay ethnic group concentrated in southeastern Borneo.

BILINEAL DESCENT GROUP: A type of kin group; a descent group focused on an ancestor and in which membership is transmitted from generation to generation through both men and women. Thus, such a group contains all the descendants of the focal ancestor.

BILINEAL DESCENDANTS: All the descendants of a particular progenitor, regardless of whether, in any particular generation, descent is transmitted or traced through a male or a female link.

Bumuh: A bilineal descent group containing all the descendants of a focal ancestor.

CLIENT: A class of dependent people who were satellites of, and under the protection of, free individuals or families. In former times, the client class in Padju Epat comprised debt "slaves" and prisoners of war, and their children.

COLLATERAL RELATIVES: Consanguineal relatives who are not lineal; *i.e.,* blood relatives of an individual who are neither his ancestors nor his descendants. Includes such categories as sibling, cousin, aunt, uncle, niece, and nephew.

CONSANGUINEAL RELATIVES: An individual's kinsmen with whom he shares a common ancestor, *i.e.,* his blood relatives. This class includes such categories as *lineal relatives, e.g.,* father, mother, child, grandparent, grandchild; and *collateral relatives, e.g.,* sibling, cousin, aunt, uncle, niece, nephew.

CORE KINDRED: Those members of an Ego-centric kindred for whom active membership is obligatory; failure to participate in kindred activities is negatively assessed.

CORPORATE GROUP: A social group that owns or controls common property or resources for the use or other benefit of its members. Herein I describe various kin groups as corporate: the *dangau* family, the *lewu'* family, the *bumuh*, and the *tambak* group. These should be functionally distinguished from other kin groups, such as the kindred, that are not corporate.

Dangau: A swidden house.

Dangau FAMILY: The small, economically independent family, nuclear or stem in type, that has a swidden hut as its locus.

DAYAK: According to Dutch convention, a general term for the peoples indigenous to Borneo.

DERIVATIVE *Lewu'* FAMILY: A *lewu'* family that traces its origin to another *lewu'* family. Results from the process of segmentation by which some members secede from one (originative) *lewu'* family to build a new village house and thereby establish a new (derivative) *lewu'* family.

DESCENT LINE: In general, a descent line comprises a straight line genealogy between a particular ancestor and a particular descendant formed in accordance with the rules governing the transmission of membership in a particular type of descent group. For example, in Padju Epat the rules governing the *bumuh* specify that in each generation membership is transmitted through both men and women. This is a bilineal descent rule. In accordance with this rule, a separate descent line may be traced downward from the *bumuh* progenitor, through a male or a female link in each succeeding generation, to each individual in the *bumuh*. Each would be an ambilineal descent line. The genealogical line comprising the group's custodians is one of many, albeit an important one, of the descent lines that could be identified in a *bumuh*. Conversely, looking from the bottom up, an individual wishing to demonstrate or validate his membership in a particular descent group, such as the *bumuh*, may, by applying rules congruent with those governing the transmission of descent group membership, construct a genealogical line leading upward to the group's progenitor. This would be an ascent line. In the case of the *bumuh,* it would lead from an individual upward through either a male or female link in each generation, to the group's founder. This would form an ambilineal ascent line. However, since an individual wishing to validate his membership in a *bumuh* may not remember all the people intervening between himself and the focal ancestor, it is sufficient for him to construct an ascent line to one of the individuals in the descent line of *bumuh* custodians.

DYADIC TIES: The formal and informal relationships obtaining between a pair of individuals of particular statuses. In this book we discuss the dyadic ties that govern behavior between types of kinsmen, *e.g.*, elder and younger siblings, parent and child, cousin and cousin. See also the discussion of dyadic kindred activities, p. 110 ff.

EGO-CENTRIC KINDRED: Taking a particular individual Ego as a focus, his kindred comprises, in Padju Epat, all the descendants of his eight pairs of great-great grandparents. With the exception of full siblings, no two people will have the same kindred. Although the kindreds of some individuals may overlap, the only person linking all the members of his kindred is the focal Ego. For this reason, social categories of the kindred type are frequently referred to as "Ego-centric."

ENDOFILIATION: The process or state in which an individual maintains post-marital affiliation with his natal *lewu'* family. See exofiliation.

ENDOGAMY, VILLAGE: The requirement, preference, or statistical tendency for individuals to find spouses within their natal village.

EXOFILIATION: The process or state in which an individual establishes post-marital affiliation with the *lewu'* family of his spouse. See endofiliation.

FOCAL ANCESTOR: The founder or progenitor of a descent group, such as the *bumuh.*

Gawe: A ceremony honoring the crocodile spirit Dewata, at which water guardian statues (*tungkup*) are erected.

HALAMAN: An extinct Padju Epat village, from which the present settlements were founded.

Idjambe: The traditional nine-day cremation ceremony.

Kaharingan: Animist.

KARARAT: One of Padju Epat's villages.

KINDRED: See Ego-centric kindred.

KINDRED POOL: Those members of an Ego-centric kindred for whom active membership is optional.

LABAI LUMIAH: A fanatical convert to Islam who allegedly destroyed the cremation structures in all Ma'anyan villages except those of Padju Epat.

Lewu': A village house.

Lewu' FAMILY: A kin group comprising the one or more *dangau* families that have rights in a village house. Contains the endofiliative descendants, and their spouses, of the builders of a village house.

LIFE-CYCLE CEREMONIES: Ceremonies celebrated by or for an individual at culturally defined important points in his life.

MALAY: A language originating from south Sumatra and the Malay Peninsula, that has served for centuries as a *lingua franca* in the Indonesian archipelago, and which serves as the basis for the national languages of both Indonesia and Malaysia.

MALAYS: Islamic, Malay-speaking peoples living in the Malay Peninsula and in the coastal and riverine regions of Indonesia's larger islands.

MATRILATERAL: On the mother's side. Generally, kinsmen to whom an individual traces a relationship through his mother.

MAXIMAL *Bumuh*: From a particular individual's point of view, the set of people descended from one of his pairs of great-great grandparents.

Mia: A Ma'anyan final death ceremony that does not involve cremation; practiced primarily among non-Padju Epat Ma'anyan.

Mira ka'ayat: The annual spirit propitiation ritual given after harvest.

MURUTUWU: One of Padju Epat's villages.

Nanyu': A returned ancestral spirit who offers protection to his descendants that feed him.

NUCLEAR FAMILY: Generally speaking, an economically independent domestic unit that contains only one married couple. Several varieties are found in Padju Epat: the *incomplete nuclear* family comprises a husband and wife who have not yet had children. The *complete nuclear* family contains a husband and wife and their unmarried children. The *reduced nuclear* family comprises a husband and wife alone, all children having seceded from the unit. These are not static structural types, but represent phases in the corporate life cycle of individual *dangau* families. See stem family.

ORIGINATIVE *Lewu'* FAMILY: A *lewu'* family from which some members have seceded to build a new village house and, thereby, establish a new (derivative) *lewu'* family.

PADJU SAPULUH: The "Ten Villages," one of the three main subgroups of the Ma'anyan tribe. The traditional territory of the Padju Sapuluh settlements lies to the south and east of Padju Epat, in the upper reaches of the Patai River. Tamiang Layang is the most important of the Padju Sapuluh settlements. Tamiang Layang is a market center in the periodic market system and is also the seat of government for the district in which both Padju Epat and Padju Sapuluh lie.

Papuian: The cremation structure used in *idjambe*.

PATRILATERAL: On the father's side. Generally, kinsmen to whom an individual traces a relationship through his father.

Pilah: In animist ceremonies, the purificatory spattering of people or objects with the blood of a sacrificial animal.

PIONEER: That individual who first clears the virgin forest from a particular plot of land.

PIONEER USE RIGHTS: The exclusive rights to the use of a particular plot of land that accrue to the person (pioneer) who first clears the virgin forest from the plot.

PROGENITOR: The founder or focal ancestor of a descent group, such as the *bumuh*.

RESIDENCE: The place where one resides. One of the most important elements determining an individual's membership in certain kin groups, such as the *dangau* family and the *lewu'* family.

SARUNAI: The legendary homeland of the Ma'anyan in southeastern Borneo.

SHAMAN: A professional religious specialist who can communicate with the spirit world, and who serves the community as ritual expert, doctor, historian, and entertainer.

SIONG: One of Padju Epat's villages.

STEM FAMILY: Generally speaking, an economically independent domestic unit that contains one, and only one, conjugal unit (a married couple or the surviving spouse of a married pair) in each of at least two successive generations. Several varieties may be recognized in Padju Epat, of which the most important are:

The *complete stem* family, comprising a husband and wife, their unmarried children, plus one married child and the latter's spouse and children;

The *broken stem* family, comprising a husband and wife, a single aged parent of one of the spouses, plus the couple's children.

These are not static structural types, but represent phases in the corporate life cycle of individual *dangau* families. See nuclear family.

SWIDDEN: A term denoting the practice of shifting, slash, and burn agriculture in which new fields (swiddens) are generally cleared from the forest each year, burned over and planted in crops, and in which a single plot (swidden) rarely is used for more than one or two years, after which it is allowed to lie fallow for a number of years while the forest regenerates itself. In Padju Epat the main crop in the swidden system is dry rice, with various fruits, vegetables, and sugarcane serving as secondary crops. The term also is used frequently to denote a field under swidden cultivation.

Tambak: An elevated, ornately carved ironwood box into which the ashes of the dead are placed following cremation.

Tambak GROUP: A kin group having a *tambak* as its locus; contains all the endofiliative descendants and their spouses of a *tambak*'s founder.

TAMPULANGIT: A Bandjar Malay village located in Padju Epat.

TELANG: One of Padju Epat's villages; the administrative and economic center of the subdistrict.

TEKNONYMY: The practice by which an individual takes his name (teknonym) from the name of a child, and is referred to and addressed as the parent of that child. In Padju Epat, teknonyms are also taken from grandchildren.

UXORILOCAL RESIDENCE: The practice by which a couple takes up post-marital residence with the family of the wife.

VIRILOCAL RESIDENCE: The practice by which a couple takes up post-marital residence with the family of the husband.

A Note on Orthography

Consonants	Represents
tj	voiceless palatal affricate
dj	voiced palatal affricate
ny	voiced palatal nasal
ng	voiced velar nasal
w	voiced bilabial spirant
'	glottal stop

Other consonantal symbols represent the same general sounds as do the corresponding English orthographic symbols.

Vowels	Represents
i	high front unrounded vowel
u	high back rounded vowel
e	mid front vowel
o	mid back vowel
a	low central vowel